KU-071-415

Satire

**Jane Ogborn
and Peter Buckroyd**

WITHDRAWN

Series Editor: Adrian Barlow

EG15344

CAMBRIDGE UNIVERSITY PRESS

PUBLISHED BY THE PRESS SYNDICATE OF THE UNIVERSITY OF CAMBRIDGE
The Pitt Building, Trumpington Street, Cambridge, United Kingdom

CAMBRIDGE UNIVERSITY PRESS
The Edinburgh Building, Cambridge CB2 2RU, UK
40 West 20th Street, New York, NY 10011–4211, USA
10 Stamford Road, Oakleigh, VIC 3166, Australia
Ruiz de Alarcón 13, 28014 Madrid, Spain
Dock House, The Waterfront, Cape Town 8001, South Africa

http://www.cambridge.org

© Cambridge University Press 2001

This book is in copyright. Subject to statutory exception and to the provisions of
relevant collective licensing agreements, no reproduction of any part may take
place without the written permission of Cambridge University Press.

First published 2001

Printed in the United Kingdom at the University Press, Cambridge

Typefaces: Clearface and Mixage   *System:* QuarkXPress® 4.1

A catalogue record for this book is available from the British Library

E9 15344

EALING TERTIARY COLLEGE
LEARNING RESOURCE CENTRE - EALING GREEN

ISBN 0 521 78791 2 paperback

Prepared for publication by Gill Stacey
Designed by Tattersall Hammarling & Silk
Cover illustration: Private Collection/The Stapleton Collection/Bridgeman Art
Library, London. *Welladay! Is this my Son Tom*, from an original drawing by
Grimm, printed for Carington Bowles, London, published 1773 (litho) by English
School (18th century).

Contents

Time line

Century	Period	Writer
14th C	*Middle Ages*	Geoffrey Chaucer (1342?–1400)
15th/16th C	*The Renaissance* *Elizabethan Age* Elizabeth I (1558–1603)	John Skelton (1460?–1529) Ben Jonson (1572–1637)
17th C	*Jacobean* James I (1603–1625) *Civil War* (1642–1648) *Cromwell and the* *Commonwealth* (1649–1660) *Restoration* Charles II (1660–1685)	John Dryden (1631–1700) William Congreve (1670–1729)
18th C	*The Augustan Age* *Georgian*	Jonathan Swift (1667–1745) Alexander Pope (1688–1744) William Hogarth (1697–1764)
19th C	*Regency* *Romantics* *Victorians* Queen Victoria (1837–1901)	Jane Austen (1775–1817) Lord Byron (1788–1824) Charles Dickens (1812–1870) Arthur Hugh Clough (1819–1861) Mark Twain (1835–1910)
20th C		E.E. Cummings (1894–1962) Evelyn Waugh (1903–1966) Joseph Heller (1923–1999) Carol Ann Duffy Steve Bell

Genre	Extract in Part 3 from
poetry	*The Canterbury Tales* (1387–1392) from The General Prologue
poetry	*Colin Clout* (1522)
drama	*The Alchemist* (1610)
poetry	*Absalom and Achitophel* (1682)
drama	*The Way of the World* (1700)
prose	'A Meditation upon a Broomstick' (1704)
	Gulliver's Travels (1726)
	A Modest Proposal (1729)
poetry	*The Rape of the Lock* (1712)
	Moral Essays: 'Epistle 4' (1732)
	'Epistle to Dr. Arbuthnot' (1735)
art	*Marriage A-la-Mode* (1743)
prose	*Northanger Abbey* (1818)
poetry	*Don Juan* Canto I (1819)
prose	*Bleak House* (1853)
poetry	'The Latest Decalogue' (1862)
prose	*Huckleberry Finn* (1885)
poetry	'next to of course god'
	'a salesman is an it'
	'ygUDuh' (1941)
prose	*Decline and Fall* (1928)
prose	*Catch-22* (1961)
poetry	'Poet for Our Times' (1990)
	'Making Money' (1990)
cartoon	'Righty Ho!' (1993)

Introduction

The aim of this book is to help students to become more aware of how understanding something about the contexts – literary, linguistic, social, historical or cultural – in which any text is produced can enhance their reading and help them to develop their own informed interpretations of what they read.

The extracts chosen for Part 3: Texts and extracts attempt to provide a broad historical map of satire in English literature, from Chaucer to the present day. The Time line (see pages 6–7) provides a framework for placing in context each of the extracts included in Part 3.

The focus of this book is on satire – a particular kind of writing which initially appears more dependent than most on the historical or social context in which it was produced. However, this book also aims to consider other contexts in which texts are written and read. These contexts relate to a text's genre, its language, its author and its reader. Through information about, and discussion of, the extracts in Part 3, the book aims to demonstrate the value to a reader of asking the following groups of questions in order to put a text into context.

About the genre and language

- Is this text prose fiction, poetry, drama or literary non-fiction?

- What is interesting about the ways the writer is using language?

- How does it relate to other texts of a similar kind (for example, other sonnets), or other texts which belong to a similar group (for example, the work of other Romantic poets)?

- What references to, or borrowings from, other texts of different kinds does it make?

These questions are addressed in Part 1: Approaching the subject and Part 2: Approaching the texts, and also in the background notes to each extract. The first two questions focus on any single text. Answering them needs careful reading and commentary on the writer's style and linguistic choices, and the form and structure of the text, all of which reflect the period in which it was written. The third question begins to extend the context by relating the single text to a wider range of other literature.

About the author

- Who wrote this text and when?
- What else did this writer read and write?
- What is the writer's race, gender and social class?

These questions are mainly addressed in the background notes to the extracts. It is not necessary to know a writer's biography in order to respond to their writing, but placing a text in the context of the rest of their work can help in identifying characteristics of their style, and understanding their subject matter and themes better. Knowledge about the author's race, gender or social class can also cast light on the treatment of these in their writing.

About the period

- When was this text written?
- What does it tell a reader about the history, politics or culture of its period?
- What more does a reader need to know about these subjects in order to understand the text more fully?

These questions are addressed partly in the background notes, and partly in Parts 1 and 2. The first question sees the text as something which is created at a particular time, and which reflects that. The second question is about the information regarding uses of language, time and setting which are woven into the text, so that, in the course of reading a novel or poem, or watching a play, that text teaches the reader and audience what they need to know. The third refers to what is often called 'background knowledge', extra contextual knowledge which can deepen understanding still further.

About the reader

- How am I arriving at my view of this text, and its possible meanings?
- How have other readers responded to the text since it was first published?

These questions are addressed in Part 4: Critical approaches. The first question draws attention to the part the reader plays in responding to the text, and interpreting it in the context of his or her own experience. The second places the individual reader and the text in the wider context of how it has been read and discussed over time.

The process of putting a text into its context is not a matter of routine. Different texts will dictate the most useful and relevant way of starting off, by making the reader ask questions about unfamiliar subject matter, vocabulary, references and allusions. Some of these will lead to historical or biographical research; some will lead back into the text itself and its relationship with other literary works. Whichever direction the reading takes, the contexts of any text will always involve the writer and the reader and will provide answers to questions about how, when, where and by whom a text is produced and also about how, when, where and by whom it is read.

How this book is organised

Part 1: Approaching the subject
Part 1 discusses the nature of satire, looking at its origins and development in English literature, and goes on to examine the different types of contexts important in understanding satire.

Part 2: Approaching the texts
Part 2 considers the most useful kinds of contextual knowledge needed to read and write about a range of satirical texts.

Part 3: Texts and extracts
Part 3 contains texts and extracts discussed in the rest of the book, or used as the focus for tasks or assignments. Each extract is introduced by background notes on the writer and the text.

Part 4: Critical approaches
Part 4 examines the relationship of both writer and reader to a text, and goes on to explore the different ways in which critics have reacted to some key satirical texts.

Part 5: How to write about satirical texts
Part 5 offers guidelines and assignments for those for whom this book is chiefly intended: students covering the topic as part of an advanced course in literary studies.

Part 6: Resources
This part contains satire 'trails', together with guidance on further reading, and a glossary and index.

At different points throughout the book, and at the end of Parts 1, 2, 4 and 5 there are tasks and assignments, designed to help the reader reflect on ideas discussed in the text.

1 | Approaching the subject

- What is satire?

- Where does satire come from?

- Is satire a genre?

- Does satire always stand the test of time?

- What does reading and writing about satire involve?

- How important are different kinds of context to understanding satire?

What is satire?

What distinguishes satire from other kinds of writing, whether its prevailing tone is comic or more serious, is the moral purpose of the satirist – the desire to 'mend the world'. The author, the playwright, the scriptwriter, the impersonator, or the stand-up comic has a view of how people and society should behave morally, and contrasts this with what he or she sees as the vices and follies of the time. This is also true of the producers of visual as well as written texts, for example in the work of the 18th-century artist, William Hogarth (1697–1764); the political cartoonists and caricaturists, Thomas Rowlandson (1756–1827), James Gillray (1757–1815) and George Cruikshank (1792–1878); or Steve Bell at the end of the 20th century.

It is possible to begin to establish some definitions of satire as a written form through the following quotations from the work of writers during the great age of satire, the 18th century:

> 'Tis the intent and business of the stage,
> To copy out the follies of the age,
> To hold to every man a faithful glass,
> And show him of what species he's an ass.
> (John Vanburgh *The Provoked Wife*, first performed 1697)

> Satire, being levelled at all, is never resented for an offence by any.
> (Jonathan Swift Preface *Tale of a Tub*, 1704)

> Satire is a sort of glass, wherein beholders do generally discover everybody's face but their own.
> (Jonathan Swift Preface *Battle of the Books*, 1704)

There are two ends that men propose in writing satire, one of them less novel than the other, as regarding nothing further than personal satisfaction, and pleasure of the writer, but without any view towards personal malice; the other is a public spirit, prompting men of genius and virtue, to mend the world as far as they are able.

(Jonathan Swift 'A Vindication of Mr Gay and *The Beggar's Opera*', 1728)

... with a moral view design'd
to cure the vices of mankind

... Yet malice never was his aim;
He lash'd the vice, but spared the name;
No individual could resent,
Where thousands equally were meant
His satire points at no defect,
But what all mortals may correct.

(Jonathan Swift 'On the Death of Dr Swift', 1731)

There is not in the world a greater error than that which fools are so apt to fall into, and knaves with good reason to encourage, than the mistaking a Satirist for a Libeller; whereas to a true Satirist nothing is so odious as a Libeller, for the same reason as to a man truely virtuous nothing is so hateful as a hypocrite.

(Alexander Pope 'Satires & Epistles of Horace Imitated', 1733–1738)

Whether or not these writers bear out their own definitions every time in their own work, there are some clear common threads:

- satire reflects society
- satire helps people to view others differently
- one of satire's purposes is to reform or change society
- satire brings out points generally applicable to everybody
- where an individual is the satirical target, satire should not be **libellous**
- satire helps people to work out the difference between folly and vice
- satire is particularly concerned with pointing out hypocrisy
- satire has a lofty aim: to prompt the good to improve the world.

▶ Look again at the definitions of satire just quoted. What do you understand by the key terms 'folly', 'vice', 'virtue' and 'hypocrisy'?

The definition of satire

The term 'satire' is thought to come from the Latin word *satura*, originally meaning the vessel used for carrying harvest produce. As so often with derivations, the connection between a word and the literary **form** being described seems remote. By extension, the word also came to mean a mixture, and then a mixed sort of entertainment, of the kinds people might have at harvest time, with songs and jokes and other kinds of humour. So satire is related to comedy which focuses on people and their behaviour.

A focus on human behaviour has been a feature of English satire from medieval times to the present day. In medieval morality plays the characters represent abstract qualities, vices or virtues, and not individuals; these plays tend to be serious and **didactic** in tone. The method of seeing characters as representative of different types of human behaviour as well as as individuals, combined with a humorous approach, can be traced through Chaucer's attitude to his characters in *The Canterbury Tales*, to Ben Jonson's portrayals of types in his plays, the typical characters of Restoration comedy, the use which Victorian novelists like Dickens make of types and **caricatures** for social comment, to playwrights like Caryl Churchill and Alan Ayckbourn in modern theatre, and to popular television comedies.

▶ Types, typical characters, caricatures: compare the passages from Ben Jonson and Charles Dickens (Part 3, pages 39–41 and pages 72–75) and decide whether it is useful to distinguish between these three ways of classifying people in satirical writing.

Satire in English literature

* Is satire peculiar to any particular period?

* What lines of continuity can be traced from one historical period to another?

Satire emerges and recedes in different literary periods in England. Its dominant period was the 18th century – the golden age of satirical writing. Major satirical works were of course also produced in the Middle Ages, the 19th century and 20th century alongside other kinds of poetry, drama and prose.

Satire in English literature is usually traced back to the Romans, and in particular to the work of the poets Juvenal and Horace. Both wrote critically about their own times, though in different tones: Horace is usually characterised as being more urbane and witty, Juvenal as being more savage and critical. For these writers a 'satire' was a particular sort of poem, with a strict form and specific content: this definition of a satire persisted in English literature in the work of John Donne, John Dryden, Alexander Pope and Dr Johnson. In any kind of satirical writing what is valued is 'wit', sharpness of observation and cleverness with language – this gives the work a cutting edge, which can amuse and entertain while it criticises.

The progress of satire

The Renaissance (meaning rebirth) is the name given to the period of European history which stretches from approximately 1450 to 1600. It is a period of 'rebirth' because during this time scholars, especially in Europe, rediscovered Greek and Roman culture, and began to read classical authors for their own sake, as literature. In England, the Renaissance is usually seen as encompassing the reigns of Henry VIII, Elizabeth I and James I, the poetry of Spenser, the plays of Shakespeare and Marlowe, the Jacobean tragedies of Webster, the poetry of Milton and Donne.

From the Renaissance onwards, the works of Horace and Juvenal, along with those of the other great Greek and Roman authors, including Homer, Virgil and Ovid, were the set books in an educated person's reading. Caxton's introduction of printing into England in 1478 had an enormous influence on the availability of the work of Chaucer and other English, European and classic authors. However, with the exception of Ben Jonson's plays, it is not a period known primarily for its production of satire.

In contrast the 100 years from 1660, beginning with the Restoration, are recognised as the key period of English satirical writing. It encompasses the Augustan age, so called in imitation of the period in ancient Rome when Augustus Caesar was the first emperor and which was considered to be the greatest period of Latin literature. Many English writers produced their own translations or versions of classic works, including the satires of Horace and Juvenal. The influence of the classics on the writers of the period, in the poetry of Dryden, Pope and Johnson especially, is very clear. For example, the 'Epistle to Arbuthnot' is Alexander Pope's Prologue to his own imitation of Horace's satires, and Dr Johnson based his 'London' (1738) and 'The Vanity of Human Wishes' (1749) on Juvenal's Satires 3 and 10 respectively.

The 18th century also saw the development of prose satire, most powerfully in the work of Jonathan Swift (1667–1745). It would probably be impossible to find a satirist writing after the publication of *Gulliver's Travels* or *A Modest Proposal for Preventing the Children of Ireland from being a Burden to their Parents or Country* who has not been influenced by his work.

In prose, the strands of comedy and moral purpose come together later in the work of many 19th-century and 20th-century novelists. Even where satire may not be the prime purpose of the text, as for example in Charles Dickens' *Bleak House*, the satirical portrayal of a minor character such as Mr Turveydrop contributes to the novel's main themes of exposing selfishness, hypocrisy and the exploitation of others.

In the 20th century, Aldous Huxley and Evelyn Waugh use satire as the vehicle for social comment. In *Animal Farm* and *Nineteen Eighty Four* George Orwell uses satire for political commentary, and to warn of future danger rather than trying to effect moral improvement.

The 18th century as the 'golden age' of satirical writing

A possible reason for the predominance of satire throughout this time (a period also known, significantly, as the Age of Reason), may be related to the reaction of people against the period of division and disorder they had experienced during the Civil War of the 1640s, combined with the teachings of contemporary philosophers such as Hobbes and Locke.

Thomas Hobbes (1588–1679), writing during the English Civil War, argued that human society is governed by two major concerns, both at the individual and at the political level: fear and the desire for power. This was a more cynical view than John Locke's (1632–1704). Both believed in the need for a 'social contract' and responsible government, but whereas Hobbes thought that it was necessary to prevent war and violence, Locke thought that human beings were predominantly reasoning creatures, and that society would therefore spontaneously be governed by civilised rules and would naturally seek order and harmony.

Whether people took Hobbes' pessimistic view of society, or Locke's optimistic one, satire became a necessary and effective method of drawing attention to the ways in which human behaviour falls short of its ideal, and of trying to correct that, within an accepted political and social framework. 'To cure the vices of mankind', as Jonathan Swift put it, became the job of the satirist. It is this moral purpose which underlies all the great satirical achievements of the period from the poetry of Dryden, Pope and Johnson to the paintings of William Hogarth.

▶ Compare the extract from Dryden's *Absalom and Achitophel* and Swift's 'A Meditation upon a Broomstick' (Part 3, pages 43–44 and pages 49–50). How clear is the underlying moral purpose in each passage?

Satire as a literary genre

- Is satire a **genre** in its own right, or is it one of the methods available to a writer?

- Can satire appear in any literary form: prose, poetry or drama?

The broad outline of the origins and development of satire given above and sketched in the Time line (see pages 6–7) may suggest that some satire in English literature (for example, Pope's 'Epistle to Dr. Arbuthnot' or Johnson's 'Vanity of Human Wishes', imitating the forms established by classical authors) is a poetic genre in its own right, like the **epic** or the lyric. But satire can also be a larger literary genre, like the thriller, the romance or the western, and it can be produced in any literary form: prose, poetry or drama.

The writer's purpose for the text as a whole determines whether the satire is genre or method. If, as in the case of Jonathan Swift, the purpose is clearly to expose human weakness and folly, most specifically the political, legal, religious, scientific and social weaknesses, follies and abuses of 18th-century England, as he does in *Gulliver's Travels*, then the text is a satire. It is not a novel, a travelogue or an autobiography, although all those forms of prose are called into play as part of it. If, as in Charles Dickens (1812–1870), the development of themes through the telling of the story and the interplay of characters is more important, then satire is a part of the writer's method rather than the prime motive for the text.

▶ Make a list of the satirical texts with which you are familiar. How easy (or helpful) do you find it to classify them under 'genre' or 'method'?

Standing the test of time

The subject of the satire is likely to determine whether or not the satire has staying power. Today, most satire is found in the work of cartoonists, TV impersonators, stand-up comics and journalists, all of whom draw on immediate events and personalities currently well known to the public to make their points. Here the target tends to be impermanent and ephemeral – individual politicians, for example. It is good for a quick laugh, but is much less likely to endure. Satire is most likely to last when its target is some aspect of human behaviour. Carol Ann Duffy's 'Poet for Our Times' will make his point as long as the tabloid press exists, and would have been recognisable to Swift or Dickens, and perhaps even to Chaucer.

▶ Read Carol Ann Duffy's 'Poet For Our Times' (Part 3, pages 93–94). Who and what are the targets for her satire? Which do you think this poem attacks – folly or vice?

The language of satire

Apart from its moral purpose, the features which distinguish satire from other kinds of writing are its flexibility of tone, and its consistent use of wit and **irony**. The most consistent target for satire in any period is hypocrisy, and the most consistently common method which satirists employ is irony. Irony expects the reader to be always alert to the conflict between the literal and the actual meanings of what is being said. So readers need to be able to read closely, to draw inferences from a text and to make deductions, and also to make connections between the text and their own experiences.

To discuss satire a reader needs a wide vocabulary of descriptive words for the different ways in which criticism of human behaviour can be expressed: comic, humorous, sarcastic, sardonic, witty, urbane, caustic, vituperative, savage. As part of the context within which the discussion of a satire takes place, some appreciation of the different forms or styles which a satirist may choose to employ is useful, since writers often make use of different literary forms to create a comic or satirical effect through **parody** (an imitation of an original text) or **pastiche** (writing in the style of another author).

Understanding satire in different contexts

The initial impetus for a satire lies in the age in which it was written. Consequently, for readers at a later date appreciating the finer points of the contemporary references is probably always going to be as difficult as understanding why many of the jokes in Shakespeare's plays were funny at the time. However, because the satirists' purpose is to expose human hypocrisy, vice and folly, and because these aspects of human behaviour are not particular to any one historical period, readers at any subsequent moment in time can at least see the point and get the message. Knowing the specific details of when a satirical text was produced, and what the social, political or personal circumstances were which gave rise to it, can add to and deepen that understanding. But unless a reader can see how the satirist is using language to show often unpalatable truths about individuals and their society, historical detail and background information will be so much second-hand baggage.

Assignments

1   In order to experiment with the amount of contextual knowledge needed
    to appreciate a satirical text, choose a political cartoon from a recent
    newspaper. Stick the cartoon on a sheet of sugar paper. In pairs, discuss
    the images and make notes about the picture.

    What do you know already about the subject matter of the cartoon?
    Begin by labelling the parts whose significance you recognise, and
    making notes of any cultural, historical, political, social or other
    knowledge which has enabled you to see the point of the cartoon.

    What more do you need to know in order to explain more fully the point
    that this picture is making? Move on to adding questions about any other
    parts of the cartoon which you find puzzling.

    Compare your annotated cartoon with others in your group. By
    drawing on other people's knowledge and ideas try to build up:
    • a fuller picture of the contexts within which all the chosen cartoons
      exist
    • a list of questions you have found useful when reading these particular
      satirical texts.

2   Choose one extract from Part 3, written during the 'golden age' of satire,
    and read it carefully.
    • What can you establish from reading your chosen text about the
      circumstances in which it was written: references to history, society,
      culture; the subject matter; the writer's attitude to the subject?
    • How does the text tell you these things?
    • What more do you think you need to know about the contexts in which
      the text was produced?
    • What do you think are the most useful kinds of contextual knowledge for
      a reader to bring to bear on a text, or group of texts?

3   How can satirical writing have an appeal for a reader or audience
    unfamiliar with the period or circumstances in which it was created?

    Working in a group, or on your own, draw up a list of different types of
    context which could be helpful in understanding the purpose and effects
    of a work of satire. Now select from Part 3 an extract with which you are
    completely unfamiliar and research as thoroughly as you can the different
    contexts in which this passage can be placed. How far does this exercise
    increase your ability to respond with understanding to the passage?

2 | Approaching the texts

- What does 'context' mean in relation to a text (written or visual)?

- How can a reader combine knowledge of contexts with close reading?

- What are the most useful kinds of contextual knowledge for a reader to bring to bear on a text, or group of texts?

- How are contexts, subject and form linked in satirical texts?

- How do readers recognise the writer's attitude to his or her subject?

- Are 'tone' and 'mood' just different words for the same features of a text?

What does 'context' mean in relation to a text?

There is no single answer to this question. To some people 'context' simply means background information – and the older the text is (*Gulliver's Travels*, for instance) the more likely it is that this information will be historical. But the context of any text has two creators: the writer or artist, and the reader. Thus, the context is a combination of some understanding of who *produced* the text, and of when, how and where they did it, and also an awareness of who is *reading* the text, and how and when they are doing this.

Obviously, then, the context of any text will be multi-faceted. Establishing the contexts could be compared with throwing a stone into a pond: the ripples, moving out from the text itself, create a whole set of circumstances surrounding its production. Another image might be a tree: the text is what the reader sees above ground, and the different answers to when, where, how and by whom it was produced are its contextual roots.

Whatever way you choose to think about it, it will be helpful to think in terms of contexts, rather than of the context as one single element.

Combining knowledge of contexts with close reading

William Hogarth 'The Countess's Morning Levee'

Look at the painting by Hogarth and the background notes on him in Part 3, pages 60–61. The picture comes from a series entitled *Marriage A-la-Mode* and is called 'The Countess's Morning Levee'. 'Levee' is derived from the French word 'lever', meaning 'to rise'; in English the word, which is no longer much in use, meant 'receiving visitors while getting up in the morning'. This suggests that the

Countess is following the French fashion for a lady to receive guests in her bedroom while she is getting dressed. A lot of detail can be observed in this painting – and observation of this will naturally lead to some deductions, hypotheses and possible interpretations. Having looked closely at the picture, putting it into context as part of a series will help to strengthen the hunches the viewer may originally have had about the targets of Hogarth's satire. It will also increase the significance of many of the details which the artist has included.

The scene takes place in an elegant 18th-century room where the lady (the viewer learns from the title, a countess) is entertaining a group of people – almost exclusively men – while she has her hair styled for the day and completes her toilette. There is a little rattle hanging from her chair, which informs the viewer that she has a child. One of the men is singing; the man accompanying him on the flute looks like a corpse. Next to them is a fop (perhaps like one of the affected and fashionable young men about town in Pope's *The Rape of the Lock*) with an extraordinary hairdo – is his hair in curlers? – sipping a cup of coffee or chocolate, with his little finger elegantly extended.

There are two black servants, perhaps to remind the viewer that much 18th-century wealth came from slavery. The little black servant boy in exotic Eastern costume is holding a statue of Acteon, who in classical mythology was changed into a stag for watching the goddess Diana bathe naked. He is pointing at the stag's horns, a symbol of a deceived husband. The remains of a card game lie on the floor, along with a careless scatter of toys and other objects. There is a coat of arms, with a coronet, above the bed, and another coronet over the looking glass, telling the viewer that the man of the house has become an Earl. The curtains of the lady's bed are open, perhaps suggesting lasciviousness, and there are classical pictures on the wall denoting wealth. There is a screen just in case anyone should need to be hidden.

There are works of art illustrated in all the paintings in this series: in 'The Countess's Morning Levee' the erotic paintings of *Jupiter and Io* by Corregio and *Lot and his Daughters* reflect the affair that the Countess appears to be having, while the *Rape of Ganymede* reflects the sexual proclivities of the foreigners.

▶ Compare Hogarth's picture with the extract from Pope's *The Rape of the Lock* (Part 3, pages 61 and 57). In what ways can you say that the approaches of Hogarth and Pope are similar?

What deductions can be made from observation of the detail in Hogarth's painting? There is a cross section of 18th-century high society in the picture. The fashion for receiving guests at the toilette was a French fashion imported into England; Hogarth may be satirising French fashions, or he may be satirising those with the time and leisure to indulge in them. He also seems to be satirising several different kinds of ostentatious wealth, drawing attention to people's dress, furniture, pictures and servants. Most of the men appear effeminate. From their gestures and body language, people appear to be doing a great deal of posturing, and all this show and finery is set against a background of slavery. The role of culture seems to be being examined: no-one appears to be listening to the singer and the flautist, and singing and card-playing are juxtaposed. The viewer seems to be invited to ask questions about relationships between husbands and wives in this society. It is not immediately apparent which the partners are or whether the Countess's husband is present. She appears to be ignoring her guests, and is much more interested in the man lounging beside her, and his expansive gestures. Hypocrisy may be suggested by the combination of fully clothed people in the room, and the adornment of the room with erotic pictures showing a good deal of naked female flesh. The Countess's loose clothing and the open curtains round her bed may be making an ironic comment on her virtue.

Looking closely at the details of 'The Countess's Morning Levee' makes it possible to build up an interpretation of this picture as a satire on aspects of behaviour in high society in Hogarth's day. When 'The Countess's Morning Levee' is put into the context of *Marriage A-la-Mode* as a whole, the interpretation of it as a satirical text with a moral message can become even more confident. As the notes on page 60 explain, this picture is part of one of Hogarth's 'novels in paint', the fourth scene in the series of six. The pictures tell the story of a young couple, married off by their respective fathers, for money on the man's side and social status on the woman's. They have little in common, spend money recklessly, and lead trivial, immoral and increasingly doomed lives. The Earl is killed by the Countess's lover – the lounging man in 'The Countess's Morning Levee' (he is recognisable by his gown as the lawyer seen comforting her in the first picture in the series, 'The Marriage Contract') – and the Countess eventually commits suicide. The suggestions about immorality, hypocrisy and deception implied in 'The Countess's Morning Levee' are part of the **narrative** and satirical texture of the whole sequence, and its meanings.

▶ Look up the dictionary definitions of text, texture and context. How do terms such as 'satirical texture' help you in reading and responding to a text?

Contexts as keys

Perhaps the best way of looking at the relationship between contexts and texts is to see 'background information' as a series of keys which can unlock the text in different ways. These keys may be of many different kinds:

literary: knowledge of genres, for example the epic, and the **mock heroic**, which will enrich a reading of *The Rape of the Lock* and add to its humour *linguistic*: for example, the ways characters in *The Alchemist* use terms from alchemy to baffle each other and to help them con the gullible and rich; Carol Ann Duffy's use of contemporary jargon in her dramatic monologues to establish character and moral values

biographical: the place of the text within a writer's whole body of work

social and cultural: for example, the background of slavery in *The Adventures of Huckleberry Finn*

historical: for example, the building of Hampton Court Palace to inform the reading of John Skelton; the rise of totalitarianism in the 20th century in relation to *Nineteen Eighty Four*.

John Skelton *Colin Clout*

Look at the extract from Skelton's poem *Colin Clout* (Part 3, pages 37–38). A great deal can be gleaned from this extract by examining some of the contextual keys.

- The linguistic context
  The language provides a great deal of information: it establishes the tone and a strong sense of the purpose of the extract as it unfolds. This part of the poem is written in the plural, possibly to disguise the personal nature of the attack, and it becomes clear that it is about people building mansions like a royal person, imitating or competing with the king by 'building royally'. Skelton gives a clear impression of the nature of these 'mansions': they are large, high, they have a lot of decoration, and love appears to be at the centre of the mansion – perhaps lascivious love. There are also several suggestions of imprisonment, with the turrets, halls and bars. The mansions are decorated with classical images, so that the triumphs of Caesar and his motives (renown and fame) can be linked with the builder. There are curiosities there too – elephants and unicorns. It is evident that the places belong to important members of the church ('prelates of estate'). The end of the extract provides its own moral context because Skelton is much more direct in his comment at the end. Having picked up on the sarcasm of

  > That is a speculation
  > And a meet meditation
  > For prelates of estate ...

  the reader can identify that this extract from the poem has been a satirical attack. And the ending declares itself too. At the same time as these fancy mansions are being built, the 'churches cathedrall' is falling down. The ending also links up all the lascivious and sexual imagery from the rest of the extract, suggesting that the owner is building somewhere to distract his mind from worldly wantonness. The irony of this is immediately apparent – the attempt to distract himself from sex has made him fill his palace with sexy things.

Modern readers cannot really avoid being influenced to some extent by the psychoanalytic work of Sigmund Freud (1856–1939) and his theories about the role of the unconscious in concealing and revealing hidden meanings in art and literature as well as in life. Consequently, more of Skelton's sexual barbs can be identified by thinking in a post-Freudian context; not only are there images of wanton wenches in the place, but there are naked boys striding, riding upon beasts, and other phallic imagery – 'unicornes with their seemly hornes'. The whole place seems to be teeming with images of sexuality and wantonness.

- The historical context
  This helps to clarify the extract and make it more explicit. Some knowledge of the period and of Skelton and Henry VIII makes it clear that, despite the plural pronouns and verbs, this is Cardinal Wolsey, the Lord Chancellor of England, building Hampton Court to compete with the king, Henry VIII. Knowledge of the king's palaces reveals that Wolsey is imitating royal palaces like Whitehall, and that he, like Henry VIII, fills his palace with artefacts depicting classical antiquity and myth; that he is decorating the place in the latest fashion, and that he appears to have unlimited supplies of money – so much money that he can afford glass windows, which were extremely expensive at the time. A visit to Hampton Court, even today, clarifies that many of the images are in the tapestries of the *Triumphs of Caesar*, which were bought for Hampton Court, and that Wolsey's coat of arms (still present in the Clock Court) depicted a cardinal's hat and naked boys who appeared to be striding, although not on beasts – that is where the satirical touch lies.

- The religious context
  This localises and makes specific the details of the poem. Wolsey is spending all this money on Hampton Court, while the church authorities, for whom as Cardinal he was meant to be responsible, are letting St Paul's Cathedral fall down.

More detailed contemporary knowledge enables the reader to decode one of the more difficult parts of the extract to understand:

> And how Cupid shakéd
> His dart, and bent his bow
> For to shoot a crow
> At her tirly tirlow.

Jenny Crow was the name of Wolsey's mistress and Skelton's curious coinage 'tirly tirlow' hints at, without saying, which part of her anatomy Wolsey was most interested in. Cupid's dart does not appear to be aimed at her heart.

The extract becomes more satirical towards the end where the speaker or

persona of the poem, the character Colin, intervenes to comment directly. Skelton is using the narrator cleverly here, as the structure of the extract makes clear. Colin, the country bumpkin, is wide-eyed at all the amazing things in Hampton Court, and reels them off one after another in a list with lots of rhymes and without direct comment. But at the end he makes his point clear, about Wolsey's hypocrisy and sexual obsessions. Irony and satire give way by means of straightforward sarcasm to direct moral and ethical comment about the church's neglect.

▶ List the different contexts in which Skelton's poem can be read. What others might you add to this list?

Contemporary contexts

Social, historical and cultural contexts are often more obvious in works from the past, particularly from the distant past when aspects of the text such as the speech and behaviour of characters; attitudes to sex, marriage and religion; attitudes to other cultures, or to modes of expression and topical events are very different from the times in which the reader lives. Nevertheless, these same factors are equally at work in modern and contemporary texts; it is just that because readers share more of them with the writers, they tend to think about them less.

Look at all the topical references in Carol Ann Duffy's 'Poet for Our Times' (Part 3, pages 93–94). As her contemporaries, English readers currently have a clear idea what she means by 'a Daily Paper' because we can buy such things every day. The racist slang of 'EYETIE WAITER' is immediately recognisable, although in 50 years' time it may need an explanatory note. Readers can recognise an 'ENGLAND FAN' as a football supporter if they live in England, although this would be much less recognisable and comprehensible to, say, an American reader who understands 'football' to mean something different anyway. Because of the contemporary journalistic context that the language of the poem establishes, we know that 'buggers' is a loose abusive slang term, not a reference to sodomy. "TOP M P PANTIE ROMP" is recognisable because parliamentary sleaze was a characteristic of 1980s and 1990s British politics; not every English-speaking parliamentary democracy has MPs, however. We are aware that 'the Queen' refers to the British monarch, rather than to a particular kind of homosexual or to a pop group. We know what 'EASTENDERS' is because that television soap opera is still running. However, some of the references are already becoming dated. 'KINNOCK-BASHER' might need a historical and political gloss for some readers in other countries; 'MAGGIE' might soon need one too. It is likely that *'Stuff 'em! Gotcha!'* already needs an explanatory note, as that infamous headline from the Falklands War has become history for many readers.

In other words, words carry specific resonances, nuances and associations for particular times. It may well be that in 50 years' time 'Poet for Our Times' will be the least immediately comprehensible poem included in this book, particularly if by then newspapers, with their standard presentational devices, have been supplanted by other forms of news dissemination.

▶ Look closely at Carol Ann Duffy's 'Poet for Our Times' and 'Making Money' (pages 93–95). Make a list of as many of the different contexts that Duffy draws on as possible:
  • what do these reveal about British life at the end of the 20th century?
  • what is Duffy satirising?
  • how universal is her satire?
Write a series of footnotes to explain the references in the poems for a reader in 50 years' time.

Linking contexts, subject and form in satirical texts

Because the satirist's intention is to expose human folly and weakness, the writer takes a subject from what is happening in the world around, thus creating an intimate connection between content and context. For example, the dominance of the church in the lives of people in the 14th century leads Chaucer to include a pardoner in his portraits of different people connected with the church – the prioress, the monk, the friar, the clerk, the parson and the summoner – and to use him to expose hypocrisy and greed, as well as human gullibility. Mark Twain, writing five centuries later, pinpoints exactly the same vices and weaknesses, but puts them into the secular setting of the towns bordering the Mississippi river and plays on people's willingness to believe in quack medicines and the 'missionaryin' around' of apparently converted sinners. In *A Modest Proposal*, Swift reacts with savage irony to the plight of the Irish poor, whom he sees around him in Dublin every day. Pope and Dryden disguise the politicians and aristocrats of their day with classical or biblical names, but ensure that their characteristics can be recognised by readers in the know. Carol Ann Duffy and E.E.Cummings create types that a reader will recognise from his or her own experience through the jargon and colloquial expressions they use.

The satirist also chooses a **form** which will make a positive contribution to the satirical effect of their text. Almost all the extracts in Part 3 rely on elements of narrative, using situations as part of establishing characters and exposing them to the reader. A popular type of narrative for the satirist is the **picaresque**: a story, often but not always in prose, about a central character, usually until the 20th century a male character, and a series of events which happen to him, often loosely linked by the device of sending him on a journey. *Gulliver's Travels*, *Don Juan*, *The Adventures of Huckleberry Finn* and *Decline and Fall* are all examples of the picaresque. Such a structure lends itself well to satire, since the main character's reactions to the different environments and people he meets can be used to highlight the writer's criticisms of how society functions or how its members think and act.

Many extracts in Part 3 are **monologues** – a form which allows the writer to create a character, and imply a situation through direct speech. A favourite method is for the writer to create a persona through which to expose the targets of his or her criticism: Gulliver and his extreme nationalistic pride, the horribly rational approach of the proposer of *A Modest Proposal*, the inarticulate prejudices of E.E.Cummings' redneck are all examples of this. The characters' speech exposes their moral values, leaving the reader to judge the speaker in the light of his or her own sense of right or wrong. Other writers, like Byron and Jane Austen, take up the position of **omniscient narrator**, inviting the reader to stand alongside them and observe and evaluate the characters' behaviour through the writer's eyes as well as their own.

Satirical writers make considerable use of different genres of writing, often taking an earlier serious text and using it as a basis for a text which either makes fun of its subject or treats it ironically. When a text refers to, or borrows from, other texts this is one aspect of what 20th-century critics have called **intertextuality**. For example, Clough's 'The Latest Decalogue' gains its satirical impact from the way in which he opens each **couplet** with one of the Ten Commandments, and then undercuts it with a cynical comment which reveals what he thought Victorian society's real attitude to the church's teaching was. The 18th-century writers use their own and their readers' knowledge of the epic poetry of the classics, imitating its rhetorical style, full of exclamations, addresses to gods and heroes, and lengthy dramatic descriptions. But they apply this way of writing to contemporary subjects for comic effect. Pope's readers would have been familiar with the *Iliad*, the *Odyssey* and Virgil's *Aeneid*, and also with Milton's *Paradise Lost*. They would recognise the ways in which he was transforming these texts into something new and completely different in tone, much more easily than a modern reader can. In modelling *The Rape of the Lock* on the epic, Pope was not poking fun at the genre. The way he adapts its form and structure, its cast list of mortals and immortals, and its dramatic events as part of his method of satirising the world of fashion shows that he knows and understands perfectly what epic poetry is and the effects it can achieve. He then puts all those ingredients to use in his lightly satirical portrait of fashionable society, creating a parody, or stylistic imitation, of the original epics.

Dryden's poem, *Absalom and Achitophel*, is based on a biblical narrative, which gives it status and grandeur. However, unlike Milton's epic poem *Paradise Lost*, which is a serious retelling of the story of Adam and Eve in the Book of Genesis, *Absalom and Achitophel* has a political purpose. The portraits of the characters gain satirical force from the comparisons drawn with their counterparts in the Bible, as well as from Dryden's ironic tone and forceful language. Both this poem and *The*

Rape of the Lock are better described, therefore, as mock heroic.

▶ Read the extract from *Absalom and Achitophel* in Part 3, pages 43–44. What clues (linguistic and contextual) help you to identify the ironic tone here?

The verse form used by both Dryden and Pope is the **heroic couplet**, first used by Chaucer. The regular ten-syllable lines, combined with paired rhymes, are well suited to narrative and comic verse, but the couplet also gives a poet plenty of scope for precision of expression, and the elegant balancing of ideas – characteristics of the 'wit' so much admired by 18th-century readers and writers. Byron was a great admirer of Pope, but he recognised that the **ottava rima** – an eight-line **stanza**, with a concluding couplet – gave a writer great flexibility and freedom of expression. E.E.Cummings shows that even the **sonnet**, a form conventionally associated with the poetry of love and the emotions, can be used satirically.

Recognising writers' attitudes to their subject matter

• How do readers recognise the writer's attitude to his or her subject?

• Are 'tone' and 'mood' just different words for the same features of a text?

The answers to these questions lie in the reading skills outlined on page 16:

• the ability to read closely, and to read between and behind the lines

• awareness of how a writer is using language

• awareness of the gaps between the literal and the deeper meaning of the text

• awareness of how writers seem to be feeling about their subject matter, which may be different from what they say about it.

The effort to identify how one satirical text differs in tone from another puts a strain on a reader's own language resources, since it calls for a variety of words to describe nuances from the most violent and accusatory tones of abuse, vituperation or sarcasm to the more subtle tones of ridicule, teasing, wit or irony. In some cases, naming the kind of writing chosen is helpful in establishing the tone:

diatribe or **invective**: sustained and forceful verbal attacks (Pope on Sporus)

lampoon: a personal attack in verse (Dryden on Shaftesbury)

caricature: an exaggerated verbal or visual representation of a person, for comic or satirical effect (Lady Wishfort)

parody: an exaggerated imitation of a literary form or style, or of another author's work (the epic in Pope's *The Rape of the Lock*; political oratory in E.E.Cummings' 'next to of course god').

Recognising the use to which a writer is putting a certain form, like the mock heroic epic or the picaresque narrative, can be a positive advantage in pinpointing the writer's attitude to his or her subject. In some genres there may be little difference between the tone and mood of the writing, but in satirical texts there is often a significant difference between the tone of the text and the mood of its author. The bigger the gap between them, the more irony is likely to be at work.

The writer's attitude comes through the language he or she chooses to use, and also through what comes over very strongly in most of the pieces in Part 3: a writer's individual 'voice'. Here are some examples where there are differences between the tone and the mood of the text.

Chaucer's description of the Pardoner seems calm and objective, but his sharp criticism emerges through his choice of words like 'apes', to describe the parson and his people – a much more powerful and suggestive word than 'fools'.

> And thus, with feyned flaterye and japes,
> He made the person and the peple his apes.

Swift's rage and frustration in *A Modest Proposal* is barely held under by his apparently logical and reasonable proposition to eat children. It bursts out in 'Let no man talk to me of other expedients' and spills over into the list of all the actions which would indeed improve the lot of the Irish, if only they were put into practice.

> … taxing our Absentees at five Shillings a Pound: … using neither Cloaths, nor Household Furniture, except what is of our own Growth and Manufacture: … curing the Expensiveness of Pride, Vanity, Idleness, and Gaming in our Women: … teaching Landlords to have at least one Degree of Mercy towards their Tenants.

Pope's attack on Sporus – Lord Hervey – in 'Epistle to Dr. Arbuthnot' is vicious in its descriptions 'This painted child of dirt, that stinks and stings ... Half froth, half venom, spits himself abroad ...', but his polished management of the heroic couplet, and the flexibility with which he balances the lines make this poetry, not just verbal abuse.

> … Yet let me flap this bug with gilded wings,
> This painted child of dirt, that stinks and stings;
> Whose buzz the witty and the fair annoys,
> Yet wit ne'er tastes, and beauty ne'er enjoys:
> …
> Amphibious thing! that acting either part,
> The trifling head, or the corrupted heart;
> Fop at the toilet, flatterer at the board,
> Now trips a lady, and now struts a lord.

Byron's chosen form allows him to seem more relaxed and conversational than Pope, but his poetic technique in *Don Juan* is just as skilful and flexible.

> Lucretius' irreligion is too strong
>   For early stomachs to prove wholesome food.
> I can't help thinking Juvenal was wrong,
>   Although no doubt his real intent was good,
> For speaking out so plainly in his song,
>   So much indeed as to be downright rude.
> And then what proper person can be partial
> To all those nauseous epigrams of Martial?

In *Decline and Fall* Waugh calculates every effect in his satire on the public school education system: his use of euphemisms such as 'discontinued for personal reasons', the telling insertions 'photograph ... if considered advisable', and the four grades of school, all expose the expensive façade which conceals corrupt headmasters and incompetent teachers.

> Between ourselves, Llanabba hasn't a good name in the profession. We class schools, you see, into four grades: Leading School, First-rate School, Good School, and School. Frankly,' said Mr Levy, 'School is pretty bad. I think you'll find it a very suitable post. So far as I know, there are only two other candidates, and one of them is totally deaf, poor fellow.'

Other writers use different voices as part of their satirical methods. Although Mark Twain tells the whole story of Huck's adventures through Huck's voice and in his language, he also allows the Duke and the King to give themselves away entirely by what they say, and also how they say it. Carol Ann Duffy and E.E.Cummings do much the same in their poems: they include and expose the politician's use of slogans and clichés, and the phonetic transcription of crude and ignorant prejudice, or political rhetoric. The exchange of questions and answers between Yossarian and Doc Daneeka in the extract from *Catch-22* conveys brilliantly the insane logic by which wars are sustained.

What the extracts in Part 3 share is the energy and inventiveness with which the writers use language. Look at their handling of relevant detail, for example in Chaucer's catalogue of the Pardoner's appearance, professional equipment and methods of operating on a gullible public; compare this with the ways in which Twain's King and Duke make their dubious livings. Compare Pope's catalogue of the items on Belinda's dressing table, and the language of religious ritual with which he describes her toilette, with Carol Ann Duffy's ironic interweaving of tabloid press headlines with the speaker's own debased colloquialisms and slang in 'Poet for Our Times'or the effect of the number of different words for 'money' which she deploys in 'Making Money'.

▶ Where in Part 3 do you find the following satirised:
education; religion; politics; women?

What other targets for satire have you found:
- in the extracts in this book?
- in your own wider reading?

Assignments

1 Choose two or three of the texts in Part 3 (for example, Chaucer's *The Canterbury Tales*, Byron's *Don Juan*, Mark Twain's *Huckleberry Finn*) and compare the ways in which each writer uses form and language.
   How helpful in forming your own opinions of the writers' work have you found the biographical and contextual information given in the background notes in Part 3, and in the commentaries here in Part 2: Approaching the text?

2 Write a commentary on a text of your choice, showing how relevant knowledge and understanding of the historical, social or cultural contexts in which it was written have helped you to understand and interpret it more fully.

3 Using what you have learnt from your study of extracts from Part 3, write a satire of your own. This is an opportunity to put into practice what you have learnt about uses of irony, and the creation of tone and mood through your choice of language.
   It is also an opportunity to experiment with form, either by writing a parody (a comic imitation) of a piece of literature; or by producing a pastiche (writing in the style of a chosen author) on a subject of your choice.

4 Chaucer, Dryden and Pope all write in couplets. Compare the different ways in which they use this poetic form, and analyse the different effects which they achieve in their poetry.

3 | Texts and extracts

The texts and extracts that follow have been chosen to illustrate key themes and points made elsewhere in the book, and to provide material which may be useful when working on the assignments. The items are arranged chronologically.

Geoffrey Chaucer (1342?–1400)

The exact date of Geoffrey Chaucer's birth is not known. Brought up and educated in London, he became a courtier, diplomat, senior civil servant and member of parliament during the reigns of Edward III and Richard II. He died in October 1400 and is buried in Westminster Abbey.

Chaucer read widely in Latin, French and Italian and drew on these literatures in his own writing, which included translations from French and Latin, and his version of the story of Troilus and Cressida. He was the first writer to show that English was just as fit a language for poetry as Latin or French could be. He began *The Canterbury Tales* in about 1386. This huge project, involving 30 pilgrims telling two stories each on their journeys from the Tabard Inn in Southwark to and from the shrine of St Thomas à Becket in Canterbury, was never completed, but enough survives to demonstrate fully Chaucer's skills as a poet, a storyteller and a commentator on the society of his time.

Chaucer's pilgrims represent England and the English in the Middle Ages – typical men and women of all classes and a wide range of occupations. Many of the pilgrims are connected with the Catholic church – the prioress, the monk, the friar, the parson, and the clerk, and the two lay members, the pardoner and the summoner.

A pardoner was licensed by the church to sell pardons from the Pope for sins, so preaching to congregations would be part of his work. He is introduced by Chaucer, in the General Prologue to *The Canterbury Tales*, in the same way as the other pilgrims, through a description of his appearance and an account of the way he does his job.

In the Prologue to the tale which Chaucer makes the Pardoner tell, he talks frankly about how he operates, and about the text which he uses for all his sermons, Radix malorum est Cupiditas (Greed is the root of all evil):

Therefore my theme is yet and ever was
RADIX MALORUM EST CUPIDITAS
Thus kan I preche agayn* that same vice   *against*
Which that I use, and that is avarice.

But though myself be gilty in that synne,
Yet kan I maken oother folk to twynne*   *turn
From avarice, and soore to repente.
But that is nat my principal entente;
I preche nothyng but for coveitise.

The other pilgrims ask him for a special kind of story, one with a moral message:

Telle us som moral thyng, that we may leere
Som wit, and thanne wol we gladly heere

*(Tell us something with a moral, so that we can learn
Some wisdom, and then we will listen gladly)*

In response, the Pardoner tells the story of what happens to three drunks who set out together to find and kill Death. Of course, the moral of his story is exactly the same as that of all his other sermons.

Coming from a period where there is a limited amount of information available about the range of classes and professions which Chaucer depicts, *The Canterbury Tales* are an invaluable insight into social and religious behaviour of the period. It is also a rare insight into the behaviour of, and views about the behaviour of, women. Discussing the historical and social contexts, therefore, is a common way of responding to the text, as is the more recent feminist approach (see also Part 4: Critical approaches, page 100). Chaucer's work can also be seen in the context of the English tradition of storytelling (see below) and in the formal context of his use of the **iambic pentameter** couplet, and the tonal and linguistic variety of the poetry.

Some of the elements of the extract describing the Pardoner can usefully be seen in a historical context, since knowledge of pardoners and their position in 14th-century society helps a reader to understand Chaucer's Pardoner and the ironies with which he is presented. The religious and theological context, however, transcends period. This can be seen from the following paragraph from a report, written as recently as September 1999, when the Guardian newspaper printed a small article on the *Enchiridion Indulgentiarum* (the Manual of Indulgences), newly published by the Vatican:

In older and simpler times, topping a Turk or 'the tinkle of money' in a church collecting box saved you 12 months or so in purgatory. Now, according to a revised guide to indulgences presented in the Vatican recently, the new spiritually correct protocol includes being nice to immigrants, praying ostentatiously in the office, or giving up cigarettes and alcohol. These more relevant steps in the modern world can help you get to heaven, says the *Enchiridion Indulgentiarum*.

The translation of Chaucer's text, which follows the extract, is by Nevill Coghill (1899–1980), who was Merton Professor of English Literature at Oxford from 1957 to 1966. In his version he has tried to reproduce in modern English the vitality and tone of the original text, as well as its verse form and rhyme scheme. In his Introduction to the Penguin Classics edition he comments on the pilgrims' stories and their contexts:

> The tales these pilgrims tell come from all over Europe, many of them from the works of Chaucer's near contemporaries. Some come from further afield, from the ancients and the Orient. They exemplify the whole range of contemporary European imagination, then particularly addicted to stories, especially to stories that had some sharp point and deducible maxim, moral or idea. ... It was not considered the function of a teller of stories in the fourteenth century to invent the stories he told, but to present and embellish them with all the arts of rhetoric for the purposes of entertainment and instruction.

From *The Canterbury Tales*: General Prologue (1387–1392)

With hym ther rood a gentil Pardoner
Of Rouncivale, his freend and his compeer,
That streight was comen fro the court of Rome.
Ful loude he soong "Com hider, love, to me!"
This Somonour bar to hym a stif burdoun;
Was nevere trompe of half so greet a soun.
This Pardoner hadde heer as yelow as wex,
But smothe it heeng as dooth a strike of flex;
By ounces henge his lokkes that he hadde,
And therwith he his shuldres overspradde;
But thynne it lay, by colpons oon and oon.
But hood, for jolitee, wered he noon,
For it was trussed up in his walet.
Hym thoughte he rood al of the newe jet;
Dischevelee, save his cappe, he rood al bare.
Swiche glarynge eyen hadde he as an hare.
A vernycle hadde he sowed upon his cappe.
His walet lay biforn hym in his lappe,

Bretful of pardoun, comen from Rome al hoot.
A voys he hadde as smal as hath a goot.
No berd hadde he, ne nevere sholde have;
As smothe it was as it were late shave.
I trowe he were a geldyng or a mare.
But of his craft, fro Berwyk into Ware,
Ne was ther swich another pardoner.
For in his male he hadde a pilwe-beer,
Which that he seyde was Oure Lady veyl:
He seyde he hadde a goblet of the seyl
That Seint Peter hadde, whan that he wente
Upon the see, til Jhesu Crist hym hente.
He hadde a croys of latoun ful of stones,
And in a glas he hadde pigges bones.
But with thise relikes, whan that he fond
A povre person dwellynge upon lond,
Upon a day he gat hym moore moneye
Than that the person gat in monthes tweye;
And thus, with feyned flaterye and japes,
He made the person and the peple his apes.
But trewely to tellen atte laste,
He was in chirche a noble ecclesiaste.
Wel koude he rede a lessoun or a storie,
But alderbest he song an offertorie;
For wel he wiste, whan that song was songe,
He moste preche and wel affile his tonge
To wynne silver, as he ful wel koude;
Therefore he song the murierly and loude.

He and a gentle Pardoner rode together,
A bird from Charing Cross of the same feather,
Just back from visiting the Court of Rome.
He loudly sang 'Come hither, love, come home!'
The Summoner sang deep seconds to this song,
No trumpet ever sounded half so strong.
This Pardoner had hair as yellow as wax,
Hanging down smoothly like a hank of flax.
In driblets fell his locks behind his head
Down to his shoulders which they overspread;
Thinly they fell, like rat-tails, one by one.
He wore no hood upon his head, for fun;
The hood inside his wallet had been stowed,

He aimed at riding in the latest mode;
But for a little cap his head was bare
And he had bulging eye-balls, like a hare.
He'd sewed a holy relic on his cap;
His wallet lay before him on his lap,
Brimful of pardons come from Rome, all hot.
He had the same small voice a goat has got.
His chin no beard had harboured, nor would harbour,
Smoother than ever chin was left by barber.
I judge he was a gelding, or a mare.
As to his trade, from Berwick down to Ware
There was no pardoner of equal grace,
For in his trunk he had a pillow-case
Which he asserted was Our Lady's veil.
He said he had a gobbet of the sail
Saint Peter had the time when he made bold
To walk the waves, till Jesu Christ took hold.
He had a cross of metal set with stones
And, in a glass, a rubble of pigs' bones.
And with these relics, any time he found
Some poor up-country parson to astound,
In one short day, in money down, he drew
More than the parson in a month or two,
And by his flatteries and prevarication
Made monkeys of the priest and congregation.
But still to do him justice first and last
In church he was a noble ecclesiast.
How well he read a lesson or told a story!
But best of all he sang an Offertory,
For well he knew that when that song was sung
He'd have to preach and tune his honey-tongue
And (well he could) win silver from the crowd.
That's why he sang so merrily and loud.

John Skelton (1460?–1529)

John Skelton was born in about 1460. He was recognised as a poet by being given the title of 'laureate' by Oxford University in about 1488, at which time he entered royal service. In about 1496 he became tutor to Prince Henry, the future Henry VIII, and took holy orders in 1498. In 1503 he became Rector of Diss, in Norfolk, but after Henry VIII came to the throne in 1509 he was rarely to be seen in Norfolk. Henry VIII invaded France in 1513 and Skelton wrote propaganda pieces in favour of the war effort.

During this period Thomas Wolsey rose to prominence in England. Wolsey was the son of a butcher, took holy orders and soon gained preferment in the church, becoming Archbishop of York in 1514. Wolsey was extremely ambitious and amassed a fortune. When he became Archbishop of York, he began to build a magnificent palace for himself at Hampton Court and in the following year, 1515, he became Cardinal and Lord Chancellor of England. Many at court began to see Wolsey's influence over Henry VIII as alarming, and in 1516 Skelton, remembering his strong allegiance to his old pupil, wrote a play, *Magnificence*, attacking Wolsey. This was followed in 1522 by *Colin Clout*, in which Skelton attacks the laxity of the church and in the last part launches a direct and open assault on Wolsey. It is this attack which is the extract from *Colin Clout* included opposite.

Ironically, Skelton made his peace with Wolsey in 1523 and became more religiously orthodox in his later years. He died in 1529, just after Wolsey had been forced to hand over Hampton Court to Henry VIII.

Skelton moved away from the verse forms which he inherited from mediaeval literature and, instead, developed his own style of short lines and irregular, intermittent rhymes, mixing English with Latin. In *Colin Clout* he adopts the persona of a rustic figure, Colin, who observes what he sees at court. In line with this persona, Skelton adopts a 'rough' verse form which he makes Colin describe:

> For though my rhyme be ragged
> Tattered and jagged,
> Rudely rain-beaten
> Rust and moth-eaten,
> If ye take well therewith,
> It hath in it some pith.

Skelton's verse has often been described as **occasional** (prompted by some particular occasion, situation or person) and fuelled by personal animosity and vitriol. Perhaps, though, his attitude towards Wolsey was not entirely based on personal hatred, because as soon as it became clear to Skelton that his assaults on Wolsey were not finding particular favour with Henry VIII, he abandoned his poetic persecution and instead started writing for Wolsey. After 1523 Skelton turned his satire against those he thought threatened the church and those whom he perceived to be the enemies of England.

From *Colin Clout* (1522)

Building royally
Their mansions curiously,
With turrets and with towers,
With halles and with bowers,
Stretching to the stars,
With glass windows and bars;
Hanging about the walles
Cloths of gold and palles,
Arras of rich array,
Fresh as flowers in May;
With dame Diana naked;
How lusty Venus quakéd,
And how Cupid shakéd
His dart, and bent his bow
For to shoot a crow
At her tirly tirlow;
And how Paris of Troy
Dancéd a lege de moy,
Made lusty sport and joy
With dame Helen the queen;
With such stories bydene
With Triumphs of Caesar,
And of Pompeius' war,
Of renown and of fame,
By them to get a name.
Now all the worlde stares,
How they ride in goodly chairs,
Conveyéd by elephants,
With laureate garlants,
And by unicornes
With their seemly hornes;
Upon these beastes riding,
Naked boyes striding,
With wanton wenches winking.
Now truly, to my thinking,
That is a speculation
And a meet meditation
For prelates of estate,
Their corage to abate
From worldly wantonness,
Their chambers thus to dress

With such parfitness
And all such holiness!
Howbeit they let down fall
Their churches cathedrall.

Ben Jonson (1572–1637)

Ben Jonson, poet and dramatist, was born in London. His family was poor, and working class; his stepfather was a bricklayer. Jonson was Shakespeare's contemporary, and like him he was an actor, as well as a playwright. Both wrote for the same wide and enthusiastic theatre-going audience, but Jonson's plays differ from Shakespeare's in being more deliberately realistic, and more satirical. During the 16th century and early 17th century trade with the Americas and the Far East was developing rapidly, and London was a major port and trading centre. As a consequence the middle class of merchants and professional people grew, as did the criminal underclass. These groups provided Jonson with his plots and characters, making an interesting comparison with Shakespeare, whose main characters tend to be upper, rather than middle or lower, class. Jonson's best-known, and now most frequently performed, plays – *The Alchemist*, *Volpone* and *Bartholomew Fair* – can teach audiences a good deal about what living in early 17th-century London was really like.

The Alchemist was first performed in 1610. Its plot revolves around the tricks of three crooks, who, during an outbreak of plague, take over the London house of the master of one of them and set up as alchemists. They attract a variety of clients, all of whom are easily taken in by promises that alchemy can give them what they most desire.

Some knowledge of alchemy is useful in order to appreciate the extent of the confidence tricks which the three crooks pull off at the expense of their victims. Alchemy was the mediaeval predecessor to chemistry, and was concerned with changing and transforming substances. In the extract, Mammon's question 'Is it arrived at ruby?' and Face's interruption 'Sir, I'll go look/ A little, how it heightens.' both refer to the signs that the alchemical process that is supposed to be happening in another room is reaching its climax. Alchemists devoted much energy to trying to discover the philosopher's stone, which would transform base metals into gold, and the elixir of life, which would make people immortal. Not all alchemists were crooks – some were the scientific researchers of their day, and the language of alchemy permeates much 16th- and 17th-century poetry, especially that of Donne and the metaphysical poets.

The majority of Jonson's plays are comedies; within this genre, they are a form of drama particularly associated with his name – the **comedy of humours**.

'Humour' in this sense is not necessarily anything to do with making people laugh. Although the complexity of their plots and the interactions of their characters are often funny, Jonson also had serious satirical points to make in the plays about humanity's greed and stupidity. His method of characterisation is based on different types of person, drawing on the medical and psychological theories of the four 'humours' familiar in the Middle Ages. These humours: phlegm, blood, and yellow and black bile were thought to determine temperament, depending on which of them was most dominant in a person. There are still traces of this thinking today, in the terms often used to describe people's usual ways of reacting to what happens to them:

phlegm	phlegmatic	calm, unexcitable
blood	sanguine	optimistic, confident
yellow bile (choler)	choleric	angry, quick tempered
black bile (melancholy)	melancholic	pessimistic, depressed

By the late 16th century 'humour' had come to mean a person's characteristic temperament, or the things they were especially interested in or obsessed with. In *Everyman in his Humour*, Jonson describes a humour as 'a monster bred in a man by self love and affectation, and fed by folly'. In his plays he satirises human nature, especially egotism and greed, and also his contemporary society which provided so many opportunities for 'self love, affectation and folly' to flourish.

In this extract from Act 2, Sir Epicure Mammon (whose name economically reveals what sort of person he is, socially and psychologically) is fantasising about how he will live when he is in possession of the philosopher's stone and the elixir of life, both of which the 'alchemists' claim to be on the point of producing for him. As well as satirising Sir Epicure as a greedy and conspicuous consumer, Jonson also comments ironically (in the second long speech in the extract) on the power of money, and the ease with which husbands, parents, clergyman, pillars of the community, artists and young men about town can be corrupted by it. Face is the servant who has been left in charge of the house; Surly is Sir Epicure Mammon's companion. As his name suggests, he is taciturn and grumpy. While Sir Epicure Mammon has been completely taken in by the con men, Surly is thoroughly sceptical about them.

From *The Alchemist* (1610)

MAMMON   I will have all my beds blown up, not stuffed:
Down is too hard. And then, mine oval room
Filled with such pictures as Tiberius took

From Elephantis, and dull Aretine
But coldly imitated. Then, my glasses
Cut in more subtle angles, to disperse
And multiply the figures, as I walk
Naked between my succubae. My mists
I'll have of perfume, vapoured 'bout the room
To lose ourselves in; and my baths like pits
To fall into; from whence we will come forth
And roll us dry in gossamer and roses.
(Is it arrived at ruby?) – Where I spy
A wealthy citizen or rich lawyer
Have a sublimed pure wife, unto that fellow
I'll send a thousand pound to be my cuckold.

FACE   And I shall carry it?

MAMMON   No. I'll have no bawds
But fathers and mothers. They will do it best,
Best of all others. And my flatterers
Shall be the pure and gravest of divines
That I can get for money. My mere fools,
Eloquent burgesses; and then my poets,
The same that writ so subtly of the fart,
Whom I will entertain still for that subject.
The few that would give out themselves to be
Court and town stallions, and each-where belie
Ladies who are known most innocent for them,
Those will I beg to make eunuchs of,
And they shall fan me with ten ostrich tails
Apiece, made in a plume to gather wind.
We will be brave, Puff, now we have the med'cine.
My meat shall all come in, in Indian shells,
Dishes of agate set in gold and studded
With emeralds, sapphires, hyacinths and rubies:
The tongues of carps, dormice, and camels' heels,
Boiled i' the spirit of Sol, and dissolved pearl
(Apicius' diet, 'gainst the epilepsy);
And I will eat these broths with spoons of amber,
Headed with diamond and carbuncle.
My foot-boy shall eat pheasants, calvered salmons,
Knots, godwits, lampreys; I myself will have
The beards of barbels served instead of salads;
Oiled mushrooms; and the swelling unctuous paps
Of a fat pregnant sow, newly cut off,
Dressed with an exquisite and poignant sauce;

	For which I'll say unto my cook, 'There's gold;
	Go forth, and be a knight'.
FACE	Sir, I'll go look
	A little, how it heightens.
MAMMON	Do. *[Face leaves]* My shirts
	I'll have of taffeta-sarsnet, soft and light
	As cobwebs; and for all my other raiment,
	It shall be such as might provoke the Persian,
	Were he to teach the world riot anew.
	My gloves of fishes' and birds' skins, perfumed
	With gums of paradise, and eastern air –
SURLY	And do you think to have the stone, with this?
MAMMON	No, I do think t'have all this, with the stone.

(Act 2 Scene 2)

John Dryden (1631–1700)

John Dryden was a poet, critic and dramatist. He came from a Puritan background, and his family had supported Oliver Cromwell in the Civil War against Charles I (1642–1646, 1648–1651) and during his time as Lord Protector of the Realm from 1653–1658. However, Dryden welcomed the restoration of Charles II to the throne in 1660 and was made Poet Laureate in 1668. He became a Roman Catholic on the accession of James II in 1685; on the accession to the throne of the Protestant King William III and Queen Mary in 1689, he lost his post as Laureate.

Dryden wrote his satirical poem, *Absalom and Achitophel*, in 1681–1682 at the suggestion of Charles II, with the aim of influencing public opinion about the crisis over the successor to the throne. Charles II had no legitimate son; therefore the heir to the throne was his brother, James Duke of York, a Roman Catholic. Many people were afraid that a Catholic king would threaten the Church of England and the freedom of Parliament. The Earl of Shaftesbury, the leader of the Whigs, the political group most opposed to James, had introduced bills into Parliament to exclude the Duke of York from the succession, and supported Monmouth, Charles' illegitimate son, as heir to the throne instead.

The poem takes the Biblical story of the conflict between King David and his son Absalom, and recasts the king and politicians of the late 17th century as Old Testament characters: David (Charles II); Absalom (Charles' illegitimate son, the Duke of Monmouth); Achitophel (the king's treacherous adviser – the Earl of Shaftesbury) and Zimri (the courtier – the Duke of Buckingham). Dryden uses the elements of the Biblical story, with which his readers would be familiar, for satirical purposes and gives them the pleasure of identifying recognisable contemporary figures in these critical descriptions. When describing King David, he even daringly comments on Charles' sex life, though he diplomatically makes it sound more like a compliment than a criticism:

> Then Israel's monarch after Heaven's own heart
> His vigorous warmth did variously impart
> To wives and slaves; and, wide as his command,
> Scattered his Maker's image through the land.

The verse form is the heroic couplet, which in Dryden's hands has a confident, steady rhythm. He uses regular rhymes, often monosyllables; the punctuation at the end of the lines in the portrait of Achitophel emphasises the cumulative effect of a series of self-contained accusations, and he often positions the **caesura** (the pause within the line) centrally to give the lines balance and weight.

The brief facts about Dryden's own religious background illustrate the importance of religion during the 17th century, and also how inextricably religion and politics were intertwined. The century saw the emergence of what were much later to become the two major political parties – the Whigs and the Tories.

These terms were first used during the reign of Charles II to describe two groups of politicians. Broadly speaking, Tories believed in the divine right of kings, and inherited succession to the throne. They represented 'old' money, land and property. In terms of religion, some were strongly in favour of the Anglican church, and opposed to Catholics and dissenters; others were more tolerant of religious differences. Whigs emerged as a group plotting to exclude the Catholic James II from the succession to the throne. Some were former Roundheads, others were disillusioned Cavaliers. They represented 'new' money, and held that the king ruled only by the consent of the people. They supported the claim of the Duke of Monmouth, who was executed in 1685 after an unsuccessful attempt to lead a rebellion against James.

However, in the 17th and 18th centuries the political policies of the two parties were not yet clearly defined. Both groups were split into factions, neither had a clear manifesto and individual politicians and their followers would change allegiances frequently and easily. Powerful individuals were more significant in politics at this time than any one party, and were the route by which ambitious younger men could gain public positions.

This extract from *Absalom and Achitophel* is an extended portrait of the Earl of Shaftesbury. Shaftesbury was a judge – hence the reference to 'the gown' – and in Dryden's transformation of English politics into the Biblical setting, Israel stands for England, an Abbethdin is the equivalent of the Lord Chancellor, and David stands for King Charles II.

From *Absalom and Achitophel* (1681–1682)

Some, by their monarch's fatal mercy grown,
From pardon'd rebels, kinsmen to the throne
Were raised in pow'r and public office high;
Strong bands, if bands ungrateful men could tie.
Of these the false Achitophel was first,
A name to all succeeding ages curst.
For close designs and crooked counsels fit,
Sagacious, bold, and turbulent of wit,
Restless, unfixt in principles and place,
In pow'r unpleased, impatient of disgrace,
A fiery soul, which working out its way,
Fretted the pigmy body to decay:
And o'er-informed the tenement of clay.
A daring pilot in extremity;
Pleas'd with the danger, when the waves went high
He sought the storms; but, for a calm unfit,
Would steer too nigh the sands to boast his wit.
Great wits are sure to madness near allied
And thin partitions do their bounds divide;
Else, why should he, with wealth and honour blest,
Refuse his age the needful hours of rest?
Punish a body which he could not please,
Bankrupt of life, yet prodigal of ease? ...

In friendship false, implacable in hate,
Resolv'd to ruin or to rule the state;
To compass this the triple bond he broke;
The pillars of the public safety shook,
And fitted Israel for a foreign yoke;
Then seiz'd with fear, yet still affecting fame,
Usurp'd a patriot's all-atoning name.
So easy still it proves in factious times
With public zeal to cancel private crimes:
How safe is treason and how sacred ill,
Where none can sin against the people's will,
Where crowds can wink; and no offence be known,
Since in another's guilt they find their own.
Yet, fame deserv'd, no enemy can grudge;
The statesman we abhor, but praise the judge.
In Israel's courts ne'er sat an Abbethdin
With more discerning eyes or hands more clean,

Unbrib'd, unsought, the wretched to redress;
Swift of dispatch and easy of access.
O, had he been content to serve the crown
With virtues only proper to the gown,
Or had the rankness of the soil been freed
From cockle, that opprest the noble seed,
David for him his tuneful harp had strung,
And Heav'n had wanted one immortal song.
But wild ambition loves to slide, not stand,
And fortune's ice prefers to virtue's land.
Achitophel, grown weary to possess
A lawful fame, and lazy happiness,
Disdain'd the golden fruit to gather free
And lent the crowd his arm to shake the tree.
Now, manifest of crimes, contriv'd long since,
He stood at bold defiance with his prince:
Held up the buckler of the people's cause
Against the crown; and skulk'd behind the laws.

William Congreve (1670–1729)

William Congreve was born at Bardsley, near Leeds, but was brought up in Ireland where his father was commander of an army garrison. He went to Trinity College, Dublin, where he was a fellow student of Jonathan Swift. He trained for the law at the Middle Temple in London, but soon gave that up for literature. After first publishing a novel, he turned to plays and became one of the most successful of Restoration playwrights. Perhaps his best play was *The Way of the World* (1700), from which the extract below is taken. After 1700 he wrote little for the stage. By then he was well off, holding several government posts. Towards the end of his life he went almost blind; he died after a coach accident near Bath, and is buried in Westminster Abbey.

Congreve was writing plays at a high point of controversy about the theatre. In 1698 Jeremy Collier, a clergyman and writer, published his *Short View of the Immorality and Profaneness of the English Stage*, attacking the leading playwrights of the age, including Congreve, for profanity in stage dialogue and attacks on the clergy. Congreve and Thomas D'Urfey were prosecuted as a result. It is interesting, therefore, that there are no clergymen in *The Way of the World*, and any adverse comment on the church is carefully concealed.

During the second half of the 17th century, following the restoration of Charles II to the English throne (1660–1685), literature was really an upper class culture, more so than it had been before and was to be afterwards. The plays written by Congreve and his contemporaries are known as **comedies of manners**. Unlike Ben Jonson's plays, which deal with more fundamental aspects of human behaviour, their topics are usually the behaviour of high society, and in particular the marital infidelities, the love affairs and passions of the upper classes, who conceal their intentions and pretensions behind masks of manners and conventions. Congreve, like many of the Restoration dramatists, is keen to unmask some of these pretensions and to reveal the more sinister motives which underlie the behaviour of many of his characters.

In this extract Lady Wishfort (who wishes for it!) is hoping to entrap a suitor. She is tricked by her daughter, her seeming friends and her servants, and her vanity is satirised. Lady Wishfort does not appear in the play until Act III. Her appearance heightens the comic and satirical force of the play. This is the first time the audience has seen Lady Wishfort, although it has by this point heard a good deal about her. Peg and Foible are her servants.

From *The Way of the World* (1700)

ACT III SCENE I

[A Room in Lady Wishfort's House. LADY WISHFORT *at her Toilet,* PEG *waiting]*

LADY	Merciful, no news of Foible yet?
PEG	No, Madam.
LADY	I have no more Patience – If I have not fretted my self 'till I am pale again, there's no Veracity in me. Fetch me the Red – the Red, do you hear, Sweet-heart? An errant Ash colour, as I'm a Person. Look you how this Wench stirs! Why dost thou not fetch me a little Red? Didst thou not hear me, Mopus?
PEG	The red *Ratafia* does your Ladiship mean, or the Cherry-Brandy?
LADY	*Ratafia*, Fool. No, Fool. Not the *Ratafia*, Fool – Grant me Patience! I mean the *Spanish* Paper, Idiot, Complexion Darling. Paint, Paint, Paint, dost thou understand that, Changeling, dangling thy Hands like Bobbins before thee? Why dost thou not stir, Puppet? thou wooden Thing upon Wires.
PEG	Lord, Madam, your Ladiship is so impatient – I cannot come at the Paint, Madam, Mrs Foible had lock'd it up, and carry'd the Key with her.
LADY	A Pox take you both – Fetch me the Cherry-Brandy then.

SCENE II

[LADY WISHFORT]

        I'm as pale and as faint, I look like Mrs. Qualmsick the
        Curate's Wife, that's always breeding – Wench, come,
        come, Wench, what art thou doing, Sipping? Tasting?
        Save thee, dost thou not know the Bottle?

SCENE III

[LADY WISHFORT, PEG with a Bottle and China Cup]

PEG   Madam, I was looking for a Cup.

LADY   A Cup, save thee, and what a Cup hast thou brought!
        Dost thou take me for a *Fairy*, to drink out of an *Acorn*?
        Why didst thou not bring thy Thimble? Hast thou ne'er
        a Brass-Thimble clinking in thy Pocket with a bit of
        Nutmeg? I warrant thee. Come, fill, fill. – So – again.
        See who that is – *[One knocks]* Set down the Bottle
        first. Here, here, under the Table – What, wou'dst thou
        go with the Bottle in thy Hand like a Tapster. As I'm a
        Person, this Wench has liv'd in an Inn upon the Road,
        before she came to me, like *Maritornes* the *Asturian* in
        Don Quixote. No *Foible* yet?

PEG   No Madam, Mrs Marwood.

LADY   O *Marwood*, let her come in. Come in good *Marwood*.

Jonathan Swift (1667–1745)

Jonathan Swift's family was English, but he was born and educated in Ireland. As a young man he was employed as secretary to Sir William Temple, a statesman and writer. During the reign of Queen Anne (1702–1714) he was close to Whig and Tory politicians, although he did not belong to either group exclusively. He wrote letters and pamphlets which influenced public opinion, and became friendly with many contemporary writers in London, especially Alexander Pope, Joseph Addison (a contributor to the periodicals, the *Tatler* and the *Spectator*, and co-editor of the *Spectator* with Richard Steele), and John Gay (the author of *The Beggar's Opera*). Swift had been ordained as a Church of England priest in 1694, and had hoped that Sir William and his other political patrons would help him to gain an influential position in the church or in politics. As a result of changes of power between Whigs and Tories he was disappointed, and in 1714, on the death of Queen Anne, he left England for Ireland, where he had been appointed Dean of St Patrick's Cathedral in Dublin, and where he then wrote most of his best known satirical works. He became increasingly concerned about the exploitation of the Irish by English landlords and politicians, and wrote satirical pamphlets and essays drawing attention to the poverty-stricken conditions in which many Irish people were forced to live. The best known of these is *A Modest Proposal for preventing the Children of Ireland from being a Burden to their Parents or Country* (1729).

For much of his life, Swift suffered from disabling attacks of vertigo. In later life he also suffered from increasing deafness, and in 1742, at the age of 75, he was declared 'of unsound mind and memory'. His affairs were handed over to trustees, although he was at that time still Dean of St Patrick's Cathedral. Swift became increasingly ill mentally, and he died isolated, disoriented, deaf and mad. He had always been afraid of losing his mind, and he anticipated his final days in the poem, 'On the Death of Dr Swift', written in 1731, when he was still in good health:

> Poor gentleman, he droops apace,
> You plainly find it in his face:
> That old vertigo in his head,
> Will never leave him, till he's dead:
> Besides his memory decays,
> He recollects not what he says;
> He cannot call his friends to mind;
> Forgets the place where last he dined ...

He had been appalled by the treatment of the mentally ill in institutions like Bedlam, in London, where the inmates were on show to the public, like animals in a zoo. In his will, he left his money to build and maintain a hospital in Dublin for 'idiots and lunatics' where they would be more humanely treated. St Patrick's hospital still exists today as a modern psychiatric hospital.

Swift died in 1745, aged 78. On his tomb in St Patrick's Cathedral is a Latin inscription, the translation of which is:

> Here lies the body of Jonathan Swift, Doctor of Divinity, dean of this Cathedral Church, where savage indignation can no longer lacerate his heart.
>   Go traveller, and imitate if you can one who with all his might championed liberty.

Swift is one of the greatest and most influential English satirists. His writing is full of 'savage indignation', motivated by the desire to criticise and reform society; his dominant method is his use of irony. His most famous work is *Gulliver's Travels* (1726). In this parody of popular travel writing, Swift satirises many different aspects of early 18th-century life, politics, government, law, religion, science, philosophy and education, drawing on his inside knowledge of contemporary society. Swift frequently creates a persona through whom he can reflect his criticisms, or express outrageous ideas in an apparently rational and considered manner. Gulliver is not Swift. He is a character whose love of his country and willingness to take the way things are done there at face value come into conflict with other different political and moral systems – some good and some bad, in Swift's view. The speaker in *A Modest Proposal* is not Swift. This person remains impervious to what he is proposing right to the end, unlike his creator or the reader. Swift saw one of the reasons for producing satire as 'the personal satisfaction, and pleasure of the writer' (see page 12); the energy and vigour of his language in his satirical writing makes it tempting to suppose that, as well as being a vehicle for expressing his anger, Swift's inventiveness and control of irony in his work also gave him pleasure.

Students studying history will need to clarify for themselves the differences between Whigs and Tories (see also page 42), and the constantly shifting patterns of power politics during the reign of Queen Anne. Readers of Swift, especially of Part 1 of *Gulliver's Travels*, need not worry so much about the historical details. The squabbles between the Big Endians and the Little Endians, for example, or the High Heels and Low Heels, or the descriptions of how courtiers gain 'great employments' by leaping over sticks or creeping under them, make their general party political points clearly enough. Swift's satire attacks the general flaws and failings in the workings of politicians. In the extracts from Part 2, he presents the King as rational and humane, and Gulliver as a warmongering enthusiast for modern weapons, violence and aggressive nationalism. In both cases, he gives a lasting example of how satire which stands the test of time is universal, and not specifically linked to any particular person or period. Similarly, the conditions of the Irish poor described in *A Modest Proposal* are vivid enough to make Swift's metaphor of cannibalism applicable to any colony exploited by a superior and richer power.

'A Meditation upon A Broomstick' is an example of Swift's skill at parody, and illustrates how he loved to joke and make fun as well as to criticise. Thomas Sheridan (1719- 1788) was Swift's godson and the father of Richard Sheridan, the playwright. He edited Swift's work, and wrote a biography of him in 1784. This is his account of the contexts in which 'A Meditation' was written, and also of the reactions of its readers in Lord Berkeley's household.

'In the yearly visits which he made to London, during his stay there, he passed much of his time at Lord Berkeley's, officiating as chaplain to the family, and attending Lady Berkeley in her private devotions. After which, the doctor, by her desire, used to read to her some moral or religious discourse. The countess had at this time taken a great liking to Mr. Boyle's Meditations, and was determined to go through them in that manner; but as Swift had by no means the same relish for that kind of writing which her ladyship had, he soon grew weary of the task. ... The next time he was employed in reading one of these Meditations, he took an opportunity of conveying away the book, and dexterously inserted a leaf, on which he had written his own 'Meditation on a Broomstick'; after which, he took care to have the book restored to its proper place, and in his next attendance on my lady, when he was desired to proceed to the next Meditation, Swift ... with an inflexible gravity of countenance, proceeded to read the Meditation, in the same solemn tone he had used in delivering the former. ... Soon after, some company coming in, Swift pretended business, and withdrew, foreseeing what was to follow. Lady Berkeley, full of the subject, soon entered upon the praises of those heavenly Meditations of Mr. Boyle. "But," said she, "the doctor has been just reading one to me, which has surprised me more than all the rest... I mean, that excellent Meditation on a Broomstick." The company looked at each other with some surprise, and could scarce refrain from laughing. ... One of them opened the book, and found it there indeed, but in Swift's handwriting; upon which a general burst of laughter ensued; and my lady, when the first surprise was over, enjoyed the joke as much as any of them, saying, "What a vile trick that rogue played me. But it is his way, he never balks his humour in any thing." The affair ended in a great deal of harmless mirth, and Swift, you may be sure, was not asked to proceed any farther in the Meditations.'

(Thomas Sheridan *Life of Swift*, 1784)

'A Meditation upon a Broomstick' (1704)

This single Stick, which you now behold ingloriously lying in that neglected Corner, I once knew in a flourishing State in a Forest: It was full of Sap, full of Leaves, and full of Boughs: But now, in vain does the busy Art of Man pretend to vye with Nature, by tying that wither'd Bundle of Twigs to its sapless Trunk: 'Tis now at best but the Reverse of what it was, a Tree turned upside down, the Branches on the Earth, and the Root in the Air: 'Tis now handled by every dirty Wench, condemned to do her Drudgery, and, by a capricious kind of Fate, destin'd to make other Things Clean, and be Nasty itself: At length, worn to the Stumps in the Service of the Maids, 'tis either thrown out of Doors, or condemned to the last Use of kindling a Fire. When I beheld this, I sigh'd, and said within my self, Surely mortal

Man is a Broom-stick; Nature sent him into the World strong and lusty in a thriving Condition, wearing his own Hair on his Head, the proper Branches of this Reasoning Vegetable, till the Axe of Intemperance has lopp'd off his green Boughs, and left him a wither'd Trunk: He then flies to Art, and puts on a Periwig, valuing himself upon an unnatural Bundle of Hairs, all covered with Powder that never grew on his Head; but now should this our Broom-stick pretend to enter the Scene, proud of those Birchen Spoils it never bore, and all covered with Dust, though the Sweepings of the finest Lady's Chamber, we should be apt to ridicule and despise its Vanity. Partial Judges that we are of our own Excellencies, and other Men's Defaults!

But a Broom-stick, perhaps you will say, is an Emblem of a Tree standing on its Head; and pray what is Man, but a topsy-turvy Creature, his Animal Faculties perpetually mounted on his Rational, his Head where his Heels should be, groveling on the Earth! And yet, with all his Faults, he sets up to be an universal Reformer and Corrector of Abuses, a Remover of Grievances, rakes into every Slut's Corner of Nature, bringing hidden Corruptions to the Light, and raises a mighty Dust where there was none before, sharing deeply all the while in the very same Pollutions he pretends to sweep away: His last Days are spent in Slavery to Women, and generally the least deserving; till worn to the Stumps, like his Brother Bezom, he is either kick'd out of Doors, or made use of to kindle Flames, for others to warm themselves by.

From *Gulliver's Travels* Part 2: A Voyage to Brobdingnag (1726)

During his stay in Brobdingnag, the land of the giants, Gulliver has many conversations with the King. In these he describes the English parliament, and the country's religious and legal systems, and its involvement in international politics. Chapter 6 of *Gulliver's Travels* Part 2 ends:

> … taking me into his hands, and stroking me gently, (the King) delivered himself in these words, which I shall never forget nor the manner he spoke them in: My little friend Grildrig, you have made a most admirable panegyric upon your country; you have clearly proved that ignorance, idleness, and vice, may be sometimes the only ingredients for qualifying a legislator; that laws are best explained, interpreted, and applied by those whose interest and abilities lie in perverting, confounding, and eluding them. I observe among you some lines of an institution, which in its original might have been tolerable, but these half erased, and the rest wholly blurred and

blotted by corruptions. It doth not appear from all you have said, how any one virtue is required towards the procurement of any one station among you; much less that men are ennobled on account of their virtue, that priests are advanced for their piety or learning, soldiers for their conduct or valour, judges for their integrity, senators for the love of their country, or counsellors for their wisdom. As for yourself (continued the King) who have spent the greatest part of your life in travelling, I am well disposed to hope you may hitherto have escaped many vices of your country. But by what I have gathered from your own relation, and the answers I have with much pains wringed and extorted from you, I cannot but conclude the bulk of your natives to be the most pernicious race of little odious vermin that nature ever suffered to crawl upon the surface of the earth.

Chapter 7 begins:

The Author's love of his country. He makes a proposal of much advantage to the King, which is rejected. The King's great ignorance in politics. The learning of that country very imperfect and confined. Their laws, and military affairs, and parties in the State.

Nothing but an extreme love of truth could have hindered me from concealing this part of my story. It was in vain to discover my resentments, which were always turned into ridicule; and I was forced to rest with patience while my noble and most beloved country was so injuriously treated. I am heartily sorry as any of my readers can possibly be, that such an occasion was given: but this prince happened to be so curious and inquisitive upon every particular, that it could not consist either with gratitude or good manners to refuse giving him what satisfaction I was able. Yet thus much I may be allowed to say in my own vindication, that I artfully eluded many of his questions, and gave to every point a more favourable turn by many degrees than the strictness of truth would allow.

But great allowances should be given to a King who lives wholly secluded from the rest of the world, and must therefore be altogether unacquainted with the manners and customs that most prevail in other nations; the want of which knowledge will ever produce many prejudices, and a certain narrowness of thinking, from which we and the politer countries of Europe are wholly exempted. And it would be hard indeed, if so remote a prince's notions of virtue and vice were to be offered as a standard for all mankind.

To confirm what I have now said, and further, to show the

miserable effects of a confined education, I shall here insert a passage which will hardly obtain belief. In hopes to ingratiate myself farther into his Majesty's favour, I told him of an invention discovered between three and four hundred years ago, to make a certain powder, into an heap of which the smallest spark of fire falling, would kindle the whole in a moment, although it were as big as a mountain, and make it all fly up in the air together, with a noise and agitation greater than thunder. That a proper quantity of this powder rammed into an hollow tube of brass or iron, according to its bigness, would drive a ball of iron or lead with such violence and speed, as nothing was able to sustain its force. That the largest balls thus discharged, would not only destroy whole ranks of an army at once, but batter the strongest walls to the ground, sink down ships, with a thousand men in each, to the bottom of the sea; and, when linked together by a chain, would cut through masts and rigging, divide hundreds of bodies in the middle, and lay all waste before them. That we often put this powder into large hollow balls of iron, and discharged them by an engine into some city we were besieging, which would rip up the pavements, tear the houses to pieces, burst and throw splinters on every side, dashing out the brains of all who came near. That I knew the ingredients very well, which were cheap, and common; I understood the manner of compounding them, and could direct his workmen how to make those tubes of a size proportionable to all other things in his Majesty's kingdom, and the largest need not be above an hundred foot long; twenty or thirty of which tubes, charged with the proper quantity of powder and balls, would batter down the walls of the strongest town in his dominions in a few hours, or destroy the whole metropolis, if ever it should pretend to dispute his absolute commands. This I humbly offered to his Majesty, as a small tribute of acknowledgment in return of so many marks that I had received of his royal favour and protection.

The King was struck with horror at the description I had given of those terrible engines, and the proposal I had made. He was amazed how so impotent and grovelling an insect as I (these were his expressions) could entertain such inhuman ideas, and in so familiar a manner as to appear wholly unmoved at all the scenes of blood and desolation, which I had painted as the common effects of those destructive machines, whereof he said some evil genius, enemy to mankind, must have been the first contriver. As for himself, he protested that although few things delighted him so much as new discoveries in art or in nature, yet he would rather lose half his kingdom than be privy to such a secret, which he commanded me, as I valued my life, never to mention any more.

A strange effect of narrow principles and short views! that a prince possessed of every quality which procures veneration, love and esteem; of strong parts, great wisdom, and profound learning, endued with admirable talents for government, and almost adored by his subjects, should from a nice unnecessary scruple, whereof in Europe we can have no conception, let slip an opportunity put into his hands, that would have made him absolute master of the lives, the liberties, and the fortunes of his people.

From *A Modest Proposal* (1729)

A Modest Proposal for preventing the Children of Ireland from being a Burden to their Parents or Country opens with this paragraph, which establishes the reason for the proposal, and the tone of the speaker:

It is a melancholly Object to those, who walk through this great Town or travel in the Country, when they see the Streets, the Roads and Cabbin-doors crowded with Beggars of the Female Sex, followed by three, four, or six Children, all in Rags, and importuning every Passenger for an Alms. These Mothers instead of being able to work for their honest livelyhood, are forced to employ all their time in Stroling to beg Sustenance for their helpless Infants, who, as they grow up, either turn Thieves for want of Work, or leave their dear Native Country, to fight for the Pretender in Spain, or sell themselves to the Barbadoes.

He then methodically calculates the likely numbers of children born each year to parents too poor to feed and clothe them adequately. He outlines the obstacles to finding ways in which they can earn their own keep once they are old enough – the country isn't building enough houses, or doing enough farming to provide jobs, they are not likely to be clever enough thieves before they are six years old – and then continues:

I shall now therefore humbly propose my own Thoughts, which I hope will not be liable to the least Objection.

I have been assured by a very knowing American of my acquaintance in London, that a young healthy Child well Nursed is at a year Old a most delicious, nourishing and wholesome Food, whether Stewed, Roasted, Baked, or Boiled; and I make no doubt that it will equally serve in a Fricasie or a Ragoust.

He argues through the six main advantages of his proposal, and concludes:

> I can think of no one Objection, that will possibly be raised against this Proposal, unless it should be urged, that the Number of People will be thereby much lessened in the Kingdom. This I freely own, and 'twas indeed one principal Design in offering it to the World. I desire the Reader will observe, that I calculate my Remedy for this one individual Kingdom of Ireland, and for no Other that ever was, is, or, I think, ever can be upon Earth. Therefore let no man talk to me of other Expedients: Of taxing our Absentees at five Shillings a Pound: Of using neither Cloaths, nor Household Furniture, except what is of our own Growth and Manufacture: Of utterly rejecting the Materials and Instruments that promote Foreign Luxury: Of curing the Expensiveness of Pride, Vanity, Idleness, and Gaming in our Women: Of introducing a Vein of Parcimony, Prudence and Temperance: Of learning to love our Country, wherein we differ even from Laplanders, and the Inhabitants of Topinamboo: Of quitting our Animosities, and Factions, nor act any longer like the Jews, who were murdering one another at the very Moment their City was taken: Of being a little cautious not to sell our Country and Consciences for nothing: Of teaching Landlords to have at least one Degree of Mercy towards their Tenants. Lastly, Of putting a Spirit of Honesty, Industry, and Skill into our Shop-keepers, who, if a Resolution could now be taken to buy only our Native Goods, would immediately unite to cheat and exact upon us in the Price, the Measure, and the Goodness, nor could ever yet be brought to make one fair Proposal of just Dealing, though often and earnestly invited to it.
>
> Therefore I repeat, let no Man talk to me of these and the like Expedients, till he hath at least some Glimpse of Hope, that there will ever be some hearty and sincere Attempt to put them in Practice.

Alexander Pope (1688–1744)

Alexander Pope was born in London, the son of a Roman Catholic linen draper and merchant, in the year that William and Mary succeeded to the English throne. Anti-Catholic legislation discriminated against Catholics by means of oaths and declarations which they could not in conscience take or make, thus incurring financial penalties and political disadvantages. One of these oaths was the Oath of Allegiance, which required everyone to swear allegiance to the Church of England – an oath which a Roman Catholic could not possibly take. Catholics were technically prevented from inheriting land and property, going to Oxford or Cambridge Universities, entering the legal profession or holding public office. Pope was further disadvantaged by illness and physical disability – he was very small, rarely in good health and suffered from a deformity of his spine, caused by tuberculosis of the bones. His circumstances made him vulnerable to, and sensitive about, criticisms of himself or his work.

Pope became a member of contemporary literary society in London through visiting Wills' and Button's coffee houses, where playwrights, poets and essayists met and shared their work. Here he became friendly with Wycherley and Congreve, Addison, and later Swift and Gay. The coffee houses were a particularly important 18th-century phenomenon. They provided places where men could meet informally, read newspapers, and exchange political news and gossip. Significant public figures, usually literary ones, became associated with a particular coffee house, and provided a focus for groups of like-minded friends.

Pope wrote the first version of *The Rape of the Lock* in 1712 when he was 24, expanding it for publication in 1714. The poem is based on an incident involving two wealthy Catholic families: Lord Petre stole a lock of hair from Miss Arabella Fermor, much to her annoyance. To smoothe things over between the two families, John Caryll, a friend to both, suggested that Pope should 'write a poem to make a jest of it, and laugh them together again'. This he successfully did. Pope's later work included his translation of Homer's *Iliad*, which paid well enough to make him financially independent, his versions of Horace's satires, and essays in verse on morality, literature and philosophy. Much of his work satirised contemporary figures in politics, literature and fashion, and his sharp wit made him many enemies.

Pope called *The Rape of the Lock* a heroi-comical poem. It is a mock epic, written in heroic couplets (see also Dryden, page 42). Pope's readers would have been familiar with the great classical epic poems, the *Iliad*, the *Odyssey* and Virgil's *Aeneid*, and also with Milton's *Paradise Lost*. Using the genre of the epic for his 'jest' does not mean that Pope was poking fun at the epic – he uses its form and structure, its cast list of mortals and immortals and its dramatic events as part of his method of satirising the affectations and triviality of the society people of his day. His poetic skill transforms the heroic couplet (which was the most usual poetic form in the 18th century) from what could be a monotonous and limiting form into a flexible and elegant instrument for wit, humour and satire. The first extract comes from **Canto** 1 of *The Rape of the Lock*. It describes, in dramatic language and images associated with religious rituals, Belinda, the heroine, getting up, dressing and putting on her make-up in preparation for a day of pleasure with her friends. The 'he' who warns her in a dream to 'beware of man' is Ariel, Belinda's 'watchful sprite', the worldly equivalent of her guardian angel.

The second extract is from Pope's *Moral Essays* 'Epistle 4: On the Use of Riches', published in 1732. In it, he satirises inappropriate uses of wealth, concentrating especially on the enthusiasm which rich men of the time had for building extravagant houses and for landscape gardening on a huge scale. The name 'Timon' signifies enormous wealth. It has intertextual echoes of Shakespeare's *Timon of Athens*, a play based on a rich Athenian citizen in the 5th century BC, in which Timon's initial lavish hospitality is exploited by greedy guests so that eventually he turns against humanity altogether. Pope's Timon is perhaps more closely related to Sir Epicure Mammon, with his lack of taste and passion for ostentatious expenditure. He is only redeemed by Pope's acknowledgement at the end of the Epistle that at least:

> Yet hence the poor are clothed, the hungry fed;
> Health to himself, and to his infants bread,
> The labourer bears: what his [Timon's] hard heart denies,
> His charitable vanity supplies.

The third extract is from Pope's 'Epistle to Dr. Arbuthnot', the alternative title of which is 'Prologue to the Satires'. (In this extract, the first speaker [A] is Arbuthnot, and the second speaker [P] is Pope.) Dr Arbuthnot was one of the group of friends, along with Swift and Gay, with whom Pope founded the Scriblerus Club, with the intention of writing satires on contemporary taste, learning and scientific knowledge. The 'Epistle to Dr. Arbuthnot' contains attacks on many of his contemporaries who had criticised Pope and his work. In a preliminary explanatory 'Advertisement', Pope explains that the Epistle is his attempt to defend himself and to set the record straight about his own 'writings, person, morals, and family', after attacks from 'some persons of rank and fortune'. One of these attackers was Lord Hervey (1696–1743), whose own *Memoirs* of the years between 1727 and 1737 are a satirical account of the politics and personalities of the period. Sporus was the name of one of the Emperor Nero's favourites, and Pope chooses it to add extra resonance to his insulting comments on Hervey's manners, intelligence, and ambiguous sexuality.

Despite Pope's distinction between the satirist and the libeller (see page 12), the second and third extracts show that the background to much 18th-century satire was bitter personal animosity. Feuds were carried on in public through published attacks whose language makes modern equivalents in newspapers or magazines seem inoffensive by comparison.

From *The Rape of the Lock:* Canto I (1712)

"Beware of all, but most beware of man!"
    He said; when Shock, who thought she slept too long,
Leap'd up, and waked his mistress with his tongue.
'Twas then, Belinda, if report say true,
Thy eyes first open'd on a billet-doux;
Wounds, charms, and ardours, were no sooner read,
But all the vision vanish'd from thy head.
    And now, unveil'd, the toilet stands display'd,
Each silver vase in mystic order laid.
First, robed in white, the nymph intent adores,
With head uncover'd, the cosmetic powers.
A heav'nly image in the glass appears,
To that she bends, to that her eye she rears;
Th' inferior priestess, at her altar's side,
Trembling, begins the sacred rites of pride.
Unnumber'd treasures ope at once, and here
The various offerings of the world appear;
From each she nicely culls with curious toil,
And decks the goddess with the glitt'ring spoil.
This casket India's glowing gems unlocks,
And all Arabia breathes from yonder box.
The tortoise here and elephant unite,
Transform'd to combs, the speckled and the white.
Here files of pins extend their shining rows,
Puffs, powders, patches, Bibles, billet-doux.
Now awful beauty puts on all its arms;
The fair each moment rises in her charms,
Repairs her smiles, awakens every grace,
And calls forth all the wonders of her face:
Sees by degrees a purer blush arise,
And keener lightnings quicken in her eyes.
The busy sylphs surround their darling care,
These set the head, and those divide the hair,
Some fold the sleeve, while others plait the gown;
And Betty's praised for labours not her own.

From *Moral Essays* 'Epistle 4: On the Use of Riches' (1732)

At Timon's villa let us pass a day,
Where all cry out, "What sums are thrown away!"
So proud, so grand: of that stupendous air,
Soft and agreeable come never there.
Greatness, with Timon, dwells in such a draught
As brings all Brobdignag before your thought.
To compass this, his building is a town,
His pond an ocean, his parterre a down:
Who but must laugh, the master when he sees,
A puny insect, shivering at a breeze!
Lo, what huge heaps of littleness around!
The whole, a labour'd quarry above ground,
Two cupids squirt before: a lake behind
Improves the keenness of the northern wind.
His gardens next your admiration call,
On every side you look, behold the wall!
No pleasing intricacies intervene,
No artful wildness to perplex the scene:
Grove nods at grove, each alley has a brother,
And half the platform just reflects the other.
The suffering eye inverted Nature sees,
Trees cut to statues, statues thick as trees;
With here a fountain, never to be play'd;
And there a summer-house, that knows no shade:
Here Amphitrite sails through myrtle bowers;
There gladiators fight, or die in flowers;
Unwater'd see the drooping sea-horse mourn,
And swallows roost in Nilus' dusty urn.
My Lord advances with majestic mien,
Smit with the mighty pleasure to be seen:
But soft – by regular approach – not yet –
First through the length of yon hot terrace sweat;
And when up ten steep slopes you've dragg'd your thighs,
Just at his study-door he'll bless your eyes. ...

But hark! the chiming clocks to dinner call;
A hundred footsteps scrape the marble hall:
The rich buffet well-coloured serpents grace,
And gaping Tritons spew to wash your face.
Is this a dinner? this a genial room?
No, 'tis a temple, and a hecatomb.

SATIRE

A solemn sacrifice, perform'd in state,
You drink by measure, and to minutes eat.
So quick retires each flying course, you'd swear
Sancho's dread doctor and his wand were there.
Between each act the trembling salvers ring,
From soup to sweet-wine, and God bless the king.
In plenty starving, tantalised in state,
And complaisantly help'd to all I hate,
Treated, caress'd, and tired, I take my leave,
Sick of his civil pride from morn to eve;
I curse such lavish cost, and little skill,
And swear no day was ever pass'd so ill.

From 'Epistle to Dr. Arbuthnot' (1735)

Let Sporus tremble – *A*. What? that thing of silk,
Sporus, that mere white curd of ass's milk?
Satire or sense, alas! can Sporus feel,
Who breaks a butterfly upon a wheel?
P. Yet let me flap this bug with gilded wings,
This painted child of dirt, that stinks and stings;
Whose buzz the witty and the fair annoys,
Yet wit ne'er tastes, and beauty ne'er enjoys:
So well-bred spaniels civilly delight
In mumbling of the game they dare not bite.
Eternal smiles his emptiness betray,
As shallow streams run dimpling all the way.
Whether in florid impotence he speaks,
And, as the prompter breathes, the puppet squeaks;
Or at the ear of Eve, familiar toad!
Half froth, half venom, spits himself abroad,
In puns, or politics, or tales, or lies,
Or spite, or smut, or rhymes, or blasphemies.
His wit all see-saw, between that and this,
Now high, now low, now master up, now miss,
And he himself one vile antithesis.
Amphibious thing! that acting either part,
The trifling head, or the corrupted heart;
Fop at the toilet, flatterer at the board,
Now trips a lady, and now struts a lord.
Eve's tempter thus the Rabbins have express'd,
A cherub's face, a reptile all the rest.
Beauty that shocks you, parts that none will trust,
Wit that can creep, and pride that licks the dust.

William Hogarth (1697–1764)

William Hogarth was born in 1697 near Smithfield Market in London. He came from an educated and literary family, his father being a schoolmaster who came to London to establish himself as a writer of textbooks and dictionaries. William did not stay long at school, instead serving a long apprenticeship to a silver plate engraver. He did not establish himself as an independent artist until he was in his early thirties. Hogarth began producing oil paintings in the 1720s but turned in the 1730s to what were called 'novels in paint' – series of paintings which satirised society. These paintings were stills in a narrative. Hogarth provided the raw material for a story and clear evidence of what happened at different stages of it, but he left the 'reader' to interpret the pictures, and fill in the gaps between them from experience and imagination. Hogarth therefore makes the viewers active and turns them into satirists too. He shows how easy it is to imagine and account for the loose and decadent behaviour of people in society, particularly members of the upper classes. It becomes clear when interpreting these series that thinking symbolically and metaphorically comes naturally.

The series *The Harlot's Progress* was extremely popular, but there were many pirated versions of Hogarth's work. To protect his work – and the work of other engravers – Hogarth piloted through Parliament an Act to protect copyright for engravers for the first time. This was passed in 1735 and became known as 'Hogarth's Act' – and was one of the most important things that Hogarth did for artists and writers. *The Harlot's Progress* was followed by *The Rake's Progress* and these, together with his series *Marriage A-la-Mode,* all follow a geographical journey through London, which is paralleled by a moral journey to salvation or damnation. The works, then, can be seen in geographical, moral and spiritual contexts.

Hogarth's oil paintings are the sketches for his engravings. This is the reason why, when the oil and the engraving are seen side by side, it is apparent that the engraving is a reversed left to right version of the oil. Hogarth claimed that *Marriage A-la-Mode*, of which the painting illustrated – 'The Countess's Morning Levee' – is the fourth in the series, was concerned with 'a Variety of Occurrancies in High Life'. He declared that 'none of the Characters represented shall be personal'. His engravings became popular with all classes, perhaps because Hogarth often contrasted the merchants of the City with the aristocratic fops of the West End of London so that the merchants are as much the butts of satire as the aristocrats. Engravings, which could be produced more cheaply and in larger numbers, were a way of enabling more ordinary people to own a work of art, similar to David Hockney's statements about his art – that the postcard might well endure longer and in better condition than the acrylic original.

(For a more detailed discussion of this picture, *Marriage A-la-Mode:* 'The Countess's Morning Levee', see pages 19 to 21 in Part 2: Approaching the texts.)

Jane Austen (1775–1817)

Jane Austen was a clergyman's daughter, born and brought up in Hampshire, where she lived for most of her life. She was one of a large family of five sons and two daughters; one brother became a clergyman, another a London banker and two joined the Navy. Neither she nor her sister, Cassandra, ever married. Jane Austen died aged 42 at Winchester, where she had been taken for treatment during her last illness; she is buried in the cathedral there.

Although Jane Austen's novels seem to present a narrow range of people and events, being largely concerned with prosperous middle and upper class families in provincial settings, they are full of penetrating and clear-sighted satirical observations of people's behaviour and their moral values. *Northanger Abbey* is probably one of Jane Austen's earlier novels, along with *Sense and Sensibility* and *Pride and Prejudice*. It was not accepted for publication immediately, and she revised it during the last few years of her life; it was published after her death in 1818. It is partly a satire on the popular 'gothic' romances of the time, especially those of Mrs Radcliffe. The **gothic novel** is characterised by stories that deal with the macabre and the supernatural, set in castles, ruins and graveyards, and featuring women as victims and men as their rescuers or destroyers. Modern readers of the horror novels of Stephen King, the gothic fictions of Anne Rice, of Mills and Boon romances, the work of Danielle Steele, Jackie Collins or Jilly Cooper will recognise the lasting features of these genres, and will be in a good position to appreciate Austen's jokes at their expense, and the fun she pokes at their readers.

At the time Jane Austen was writing, the novel was a relatively new literary genre and in *Northanger Abbey* she also satirises contemporary attitudes to reading, especially to reading novels rather than poetry or serious prose. While she laughs at her heroine Catherine Morland's enthusiasm for Mrs Radcliffe, she makes her own views about novels clear in an early chapter with her comments on young ladies who say of their reading 'with affected indifference, or momentary shame' "Oh! it is only a novel!"'. She plays ironically with the word 'only', saying

> … in short, only some work in which the greatest powers of the mind are displayed, in which the most thorough knowledge of human nature, the happiest delineation of its varieties, the liveliest effusions of wit and humour are conveyed to the world in the best chosen language.

Jane Austen uses satire subtly as part of the way she presents characters. Catherine's two admirers are differentiated partly through their reactions to her enthusiasm for Mrs Radcliffe's *Udolpho*, a genuine gothic novel. The boorish John Thorpe is more interested in boasting about his new horse and carriage, and brushes her off with: '*Udolpho*. Oh Lord! not I; I never read novels; I have something else to do.' The hero, Henry Tilney, on the other hand, says:

> The person ... who has not pleasure in a good novel must be intolerably stupid. I have read all of Mrs Radcliffe's works, and most of them with great pleasure. *The Mysteries of Udolpho* when I had once begun it, I could not lay down again; – I remember finishing it in two days – my hair standing on end the whole time!

Jane Austen's teasing and affectionate attitude to Catherine, an innocent, rather naive 17-year-old, is very similar to that of her hero, Henry Tilney. Before this extract begins, Henry and Catherine have met while they are both on holiday in Bath, and have already established their mutual enjoyment in reading gothic novels. In this extract, Henry, is taking Catherine to stay with his father and sister at their home, Northanger Abbey.

From *Northanger Abbey* (1818)

> – Henry drove so well, – so quietly – without making any disturbance, without parading to her, or swearing at them; so different from the only gentleman coachman whom it was in her power to compare him with! – And then his hat sat so well, and the innumerable capes of his great coat looked so becomingly important! – To be driven by him, next to being dancing with him, was certainly the greatest happiness in the world. In addition to every other delight, she had now that of listening to her own praise; of being thanked at least, on his sister's account, for her kindness in thus becoming her visitor; of hearing it ranked as real friendship, and described as creating real gratitude. His sister, he said, was uncomfortably circumstanced – she had no female companion – and, in the frequent absence of her father, was sometimes without any companion at all.
>
> 'But how can that be?' said Catherine, 'are not you with her?'
>
> 'Northanger is not more than half my home; I have an establishment at my own house in Woodston, which is nearly twenty miles from my father's, and some of my time is necessarily spent there.'
>
> 'How sorry you must be for that!'
>
> 'I am always sorry to leave Eleanor.'
>
> 'Yes; but besides your affection for her, you must be so fond of the abbey! – After being used to such a home as the abbey, an ordinary parsonage house must be very disagreeable.'
>
> He smiled and said, 'You have formed a very favourable idea of the abbey.'

'To be sure I have. Is not it a fine old place, just like what one reads about?'

'And are you prepared to encounter all the horrors that a building such as 'what one reads about' may produce? – Have you a stout heart? – Nerves fit for sliding panels and tapestry?'

'Oh! yes – I do not think I should be easily frightened, because there would be so many people in the house – and besides, it has never been uninhabited and left deserted for years, and then the family come back to it unawares, without giving any notice, as generally happens.'

'No, certainly. – We shall not have to explore our way into a hall dimly lighted by the expiring embers of a wood fire – nor be obliged to spread our beds on the floor of a room without windows, doors, or furniture. But you must be aware that when a young lady is (by whatever means) introduced into a dwelling of this kind, she is always lodged apart from the rest of the family. While they snugly repair to their own end of the house, she is formally conducted by Dorothy the ancient housekeeper up a different staircase, and along many gloomy passages, into an apartment never used since some cousin or kin died in it about twenty years before. Can you stand such a ceremony as this? Will not your mind misgive you, when you find yourself in this gloomy chamber – too lofty and extensive for you, with only the feeble rays of a single lamp to take in its size – its walls hung with tapestry exhibiting figures as large as life, and the bed, of dark green stuff or purple velvet, presenting even a funeral appearance. Will not your heart sink within you?'

'Oh! but this will not happen to me, I am sure.'

'How fearfully will you examine the furniture of your apartment! – And what will you discern? – Not tables, toilettes, wardrobes, or drawers, but on one side perhaps the remains of a broken lute, on the other a ponderous chest which no efforts can open, and over the fire-place the portrait of some handsome warrior, whose features will so incomprehensively strike you, that you will not be able to withdraw your eyes from it. Dorothy meanwhile, no less struck by your appearance, gazes on you in great agitation, and drops a few unintelligible hints. To raise your spirits, moreover, she gives you reason to suppose that the part of the abbey you inhabit is undoubtedly haunted, and informs you that you will not have a single domestic within call. With this parting cordial she curtseys off – you listen to the sound of her receding footsteps as long as the last echo can reach you- and when, with fainting spirits, you attempt to fasten your door, you discover, with increased alarm, that it has no lock.'

'Oh! Mr Tilney, how frightful. – This is just like a book! – But it cannot really happen to me. I am sure your housekeeper is not really Dorothy. – Well, what then?'

'Nothing further to alarm perhaps may occur the first night. After surmounting your *unconquerable* horror of the bed, you will retire to rest, and get a few hours' unquiet slumber. But on the second, or at farthest the *third* night after your arrival, you will probably have a violent storm. Peals of thunder so loud as to seem to shake the edifice to its foundation will roll round the neighbouring mountains – and during the frightful gusts of wind which accompany it, you will probably think you discern (for your lamp is not extinguished) one part of the hanging more violently agitated than the rest. Unable of course to repress your curiosity in so favourable a moment for indulging it, you will instantly arise, and throwing your dressing-gown around you, proceed to examine this mystery. After a very short search, you will discover a division in the tapestry so artfully constructed as to defy the minutest inspection, and on opening it, a door will immediately appear – which door being only secured by massy bars and a padlock, you will, after a few efforts, succeed in opening, – and, with your lamp in your hand, will pass through it into a small vaulted room.'

'No, indeed; I should be too much frightened to do any such thing.'

'What! not when Dorothy has given you to understand that there is a secret subterraneous communication between your apartment and the chapel of St Anthony, scarcely two miles off – Could you shrink from so simple an adventure? No, no, you will proceed into this small vaulted room, and through this into several others, without perceiving any thing very remarkable in either. In one perhaps there may be a dagger, in another a few drops of blood, and in a third the remains of some instrument of torture; but there being nothing in all this out of the common way, and your lamp being nearly exhausted, you will return towards your own apartment. In repassing through the small vaulted room, however, your eyes will be attracted towards a large, old-fashioned cabinet of ebony and gold, which, though narrowly examining the furniture before, you had passed unnoticed. Impelled by an irresistible presentiment, you will eagerly advance to it, unlock its folding doors, and search into every drawer; – but for sometime without discovering any thing of importance – perhaps nothing but a considerable hoard of diamonds. At last, however, by touching a secret spring, an inner compartment will open – a roll of paper appears: – you seize it – it contains many sheets of manuscript – you hasten with the precious treasure into your own chamber, but scarcely have you been able to decipher "Oh! thou – whomsoever thou mayst be, into whose hands these memoirs of the wretched Matilda may fall" – when your lamp suddenly expires in the socket, and leaves you in total darkness.'

'Oh! no, no – do not say so. Well, go on.'

But Henry was too much amused by the interest he had raised, to be able to carry it farther; he could no longer command solemnity either of subject or voice, and was obliged to entreat her to use her own fancy in the perusal of Matilda's woes.

Lord Byron (1788–1824)

George Gordon, 6th Lord Byron, 'mad, bad, and dangerous to know', in the words of one of his mistresses, Lady Caroline Lamb, probably has a more scandalous reputation than any other British writer except Oscar Wilde. He was born in London, and brought up by a dominating and difficult mother, whom he disliked. He compensated for the congenital lameness caused by a club foot by becoming an energetic sportsman, especially good at swimming. He was unconventional and eccentric, keeping a bear in his rooms at Cambridge, because the rules forbade keeping dogs. He was immensely attractive to women and his life was a succession of affairs; his many lovers included his half sister Augusta Leigh, Lady Caroline Lamb, Shelley's mistress Claire Clairmont, and Teresa Guiccioli, the wife of an Italian nobleman. He became famous overnight on the publication in 1812 of the first two Cantos, or sections, of his long poem, *Childe Harold's Pilgrimage*. In 1815, he married Annabella Milbanke, who thought she could reform him, but following the collapse of his marriage in 1816 he was ostracised by English society, and left England for Europe. He travelled widely, lived for much of the time in Italy, and became involved eventually in the cause of Greek independence. He is still recognised as a hero in Greece, where he died of fever at Missolonghi in 1824. His body was brought home, and buried in his family vault in Nottinghamshire; because of his reputation the church authorities had refused permission for him to be buried in Westminster Abbey, despite his status as a poet.

Byron is not easy to fit into the pigeon holes of a literary movement or group. He was a contemporary of the Romantic poets – Keats, whose work he disliked, and Shelley, who was a close friend – but he admired the work of the Augustans, especially the poetry of Pope, much more. Byron's letters convey an impression of restless activity, and of someone who pushed every aspect of his life to excess. At the same time he was also prone to fits of depression, and much of his earlier poetry is serious, and at times introspective, rather than satirical. One of his legacies to English literature is the creation of the **Byronic hero** – the product partly of Byron's own personality and life style, and partly of the characters and moods of his early poetry. This Romantic hero was described by the 19th-century writer and historian, Thomas Macaulay, as 'a man proud, moody, cynical, with defiance on his brow, and misery in his heart, a scorner of his kind, implacable in revenge, yet capable of deep and strong affection'. Readers of *Jane Eyre* or *Wuthering Heights* may recognise Rochester or Heathcliff, and also the heroes of romantic novels of the 20th century, in this description.

Byron's long, and unfinished, satirical epic poem, *Don Juan*, published between 1819 and 1824, is much closer to the Augustans in its criticisms of society and its sharp satirical eye on human weakness and folly. In the early Cantos his hero, Juan, is the antithesis of the brooding presence described above. Don Juan is the hero of many stories in French and Italian literature, which retell his adventures as a great lover. In Byron's version, Juan is, at first at least, an innocent youth, whose adventures take him all over the world, and into the hands of many different women, eventually ending up in the England of Byron's own day. This narrative structure gave Byron plenty of scope for satirising contemporary manners and society, and his chosen verse form is brilliantly adaptable to the witty, conversational and informal tone in which he does this.

The verse form is called ***ottava rima***, originally used in Italian mock heroic writing. It consists of eight-line stanzas, the first six lines rhyming alternately and then closed with a final rhyming couplet. Although this may seem a strict pattern for a poet to observe, Byron says in his Preface to his earlier narrative poem, *Childe Harold's Pilgrimage* (1812), that it allowed him to be 'either droll or pathetic, descriptive or sentimental, tender or satirical, as the humour strikes him'. By making use of conversational language, abbreviations such as 'can't' and 'don't', dashes and run on lines, and feminine (two syllable) rhymes, some of them perfectly accurate (gunnery/nunnery) and some atrociously forced (horrid one/Corydon) Byron achieves the effect of his own spontaneous, ironic witty voice, communicating with his reader with the same immediacy as in his letters to friends and colleagues. He can also use exactly the same verse form to achieve lyrical descriptive effects, which vary the tone and pace of his narrative.

Byron was initially off-hand about the overall structure of *Don Juan*, and his intentions in writing it. Essentially, it is a picaresque narrative, with all the advantages of variety of incident that implies, but writing to his publisher after the first two Cantos had been published, he says characteristically:

> You ask me for the plan of Donny Johnny: I have no plan; but I had or have materials; ... If it don't take, I will leave it off where it is, with all due respect to the Public; but if continued it must be in my own way. You might as well make Hamlet 'act mad' in a strait waistcoat as trammel my buffoonery ... Why, man. the soul of such writing is its licence ...

> You are too earnest and eager about a work never intended to be
> serious. Do you suppose that I could have any intention but to giggle
> and make giggle? – a playful satire, with as little poetry as could be
> helped, was what I meant ...
>
> (Letter to John Murray, 12 August 1819)

Yet three years later, on the point of giving up *Don Juan* for a time at the request of
his 19-year-old Italian mistress, Teresa Guiccioli, he was telling Murray that he had
plans for a huge epic involving his hero:

> I meant to take him the tour of Europe, with a proper mixture of
> siege, battle and adventure, and make him finish ... in the French
> revolution ... I meant to have made him a Cavaliere Servente in Italy,
> and a cause for divorce in England, and a sentimental Werther-faced
> man in Germany, so as to show the different ridicules in each of those
> countries, and to have displayed him gradually *gâté* [ruined, spoilt]
> and *blasé* [indifferent, couldn't care less] as he grew older, as is
> natural. But I had not quite fixed whether to make him end in Hell, or
> an unhappy marriage, not knowing which would be the severest. The
> Spanish tradition says Hell: but it is probably only an Allegory of the
> other state.
>
> (Letter to John Murray, 16 February 1821)

Byron's cosmopolitan education and existence is shown in his easy references to
Italian, German and Spanish culture, and his use of French. A *Cavaliere Servente*
was a woman's constant companion, admirer and lover, tolerated by her husband;
Werther was the hero of *The Sorrows of Young Werther* by Johann Wolfgang von
Goethe (1749–1832). This novel, in which the romantic hero eventually commits
suicide, was widely read in England as well as in other European countries.

Byron's plans for a huge epic were not carried through, and as more Cantos of
Don Juan were published he was increasingly accused of indecency in his writing
as well as in his private life. Just under two years later he wrote to Murray:

> *Don Juan* will be known by and bye for what it is intended, – a satire
> on abuses of the present states of society and not a eulogy of vice: it
> may be now and then voluptuous: I can't help that ... No girl will ever
> be seduced by reading DJ.
>
> (Letter to John Murray, 25 December 1822)

Byron is one of those writers whose biography threatens to distract readers from
his poetry. It is interesting to read his letters, not only for some insights into his
authorial intentions in writing *Don Juan*, which seem to deepen and change as he

proceeds, but also for the way they convey the personality and voice which come across so vividly in the poem itself. This extract from *Don Juan* Canto 1 describes the education which Juan's mother ensures for him after the death of his father.

From *Don Juan* Canto 1 (1819)

Sagest of women, even of widows, she
    Resolved that Juan should be quite a paragon,
And worthy of the noblest pedigree
    (His sire was of Castile, his dam from Arragon).
Then for accomplishments of chivalry,
    In case our lord the king should go to war again,
He learned the arts of riding, fencing, gunnery,
And how to scale a fortress – or a nunnery.

But that which Donna Inez most desired
    And saw into herself each day before all
The learnèd tutors whom for him she hired
    Was that his breeding should be strictly moral.
Much into all his studies she inquired,
    And so they were submitted first to her, all
Arts, sciences; no branch was made a mystery
To Juan's eyes, excepting natural history.

The languages, especially the dead,
    The sciences, and most of all the abstruse,
The arts, at least all such as could be said
    To be the most remote from common use,
In all these he was much and deeply read,
    But not a page of anything that's loose
Or hints continuation of the species
Was ever suffered, lest he should grow vicious.

His classic studies made a little puzzle,
    Because of filthy loves of gods and goddesses,
Who in the earlier ages raised a bustle,
    But never put on pantaloons or bodices.
His reverend tutors had at times a tussle,
    And for their *Aeneids*, *Iliads* and *Odysseys*
Were forced to make an odd sort of apology,
For Donna Inez dreaded the mythology.

Ovid's a rake, as half his verses show him,
    Anacreon's morals are a still worse sample,
Catullus scarcely has a decent poem,
    I don't think Sappho's ode a good example,
Although Longinus tells us there is no hymn
    Where the sublime soars forth on wings more ample,
But Virgil's songs are pure, except that horrid one
Beginning with *Formosum pastor Corydon*.

Lucretius' irreligion is too strong
    For early stomachs to prove wholesome food.
I can't help thinking Juvenal was wrong,
    Although no doubt his real intent was good,
For speaking out so plainly in his song,
    So much indeed as to be downright rude.
And then what proper person can be partial
To all those nauseous epigrams of Martial?

Juan was taught from out the best edition,
    Expurgated by learnèd men, who place
Judiciously from out the schoolboy's vision
    The grosser parts, but fearful to deface
Too much their modest bard by this omission
    And pitying sore his mutilated case,
They only add them all in an appendix,
Which saves in fact the trouble of an index,

For there we have them all at one fell swoop,
    Instead of being scattered through the pages.
They stand forth marshalled in a handsome troop
    To meet the ingenuous youth of future ages,
Till some less rigid editor shall stoop
    To call them back into their separate cages,
Instead of standing staring altogether
Like garden gods – and not so decent either.

(Stanzas 38-45)

Charles Dickens (1812–1870)

Charles Dickens was born in Portsmouth, the son of a clerk in the Navy Pay Office.
When he was ten, his father was imprisoned for debt, and Dickens had to go to
work in a blacking factory. This early experience of poverty, which he later described

vividly in his semi-autobiographical novel, *David Copperfield*, affected Dickens deeply and permanently. As a young man, Dickens initially made his living as a journalist and Parliamentary reporter and gradually became known as a writer for his short essays, or sketches, which were published in *The Monthly Magazine*. Throughout his life, Dickens had extraordinary energy and vitality. He produced 16 novels, and was also the editor of two major weekly periodicals, *Household Words* and *All the Year Round*. Dickens loved the theatre, and was himself an accomplished amateur actor. During the last years of his life he gave public readings from his novels, which were extremely popular and successful, but which demanded so much of him in performance that his health was increasingly affected.

Dickens is one of the best known and most popular of English novelists. His novels combine comedy and melodrama with social criticism and serious concern about injustice and inequality between the rich and the poor. Their immediate historical context is life in the 19th century as Dickens experienced and observed it; his novels are characterised by their huge range of characters from all classes and levels of society. Another context, which affects the form, structure and at times the content of the novels, is literary: their method of publication and the readership which this encouraged. During the 19th century the novel became a more and more popular literary genre, due partly to an increase in readers especially from the middle classes, and partly to methods of publication which made novels more easily and cheaply available. In 1821, Sir Walter Scott's publisher had been the first to market his novels in the three-volume format – a big advantage to libraries and to readers who could not afford to buy the books for themselves. At the same time, magazines and periodicals were beginning to publish novels as serials, in weekly or monthly parts. Serialisation had an effect on the form of the novel similar to that of the conventions of the soap opera on television narratives today – an episodic structure and the use of 'cliff-hangers' to mark the end of instalments. In Dickens' case, serialisation gave him close contact with his readers and their responses, which he welcomed. It did, however, also provide a cultural context which influenced the way in which Dickens presented female characters and family life, often in what modern readers consider to be a sentimental and limited way. It also affected the way he was able to deal with currently taboo subjects, such as sexuality.

This extract is taken from *Bleak House* (1852–1853). In this novel, Dickens uses two narrators: a third-person omniscient voice, and a first-person account of events from Esther Summerson, one of the characters in the story. Dickens employs satire as one element in developing the dominant themes in the novel of greed and selfishness, selflessness and love. There are a number of family groups in the novel, most of them unsatisfactory, of which the Turveydrops are one. Many of the characters are parasites who live off society, without contributing anything to it, just as Mr Turveydrop lives off his hardworking son, Prince. In this extract, Dickens' method of slipping his satirical criticisms of Mr Turveydrop's self-absorption into the gentle, generous-minded Esther Summerson's account adds to the comic effect, but also contributes to the thematic texture of the whole novel.

From *Bleak House* (1852–1853)

We went upstairs – it had been quite a fine house once, when it was anybody's business to keep it clean and fresh, and, and nobody's business to smoke in it all day – and into Mr Turveydrop's great room, which was built out into a mews at the back, and was lighted by a skylight. It was a bare, resounding room, smelling of stables; with cane forms along the walls; and the walls ornamented at regular intervals with painted lyres, and little cut-glass branches for candles, which seemed to be shedding their old-fashioned drops as other branches might shed autumn leaves. Several young lady pupils, ranging from thirteen or fourteen years of age to two or three and twenty, were assembled; and I was looking among them for their instructor, when Caddy, pinching my arm, repeated the ceremony of introduction. 'Miss Summerson, Mr Prince Turveydrop!'

I curtseyed to a little blue-eyed fair man of youthful appearance, with flaxen hair parted in the middle, and curling at the ends all round his head. He had a little fiddle, which we used to call at school a kit, under his left arm, and its little bow in the same hand. His little dancing-shoes were particularly diminutive, and he a little innocent, feminine manner, which not only appealed to me in an amiable way, but made this singular effect upon me: that I received the impression that he was like his mother, and that his mother had not been much considered or well used.

… I withdrew to a seat between Peepy (who, being well used to it, had already climbed into a corner place) and an old lady of a censorious countenance, whose two nieces were in the class, and who was very indignant with Peepy's boots. Prince Turveydrop then tinkled the strings of his kit with his fingers, and the young ladies stood up to dance. Just then, there appeared from a side door, old Mr Turveydrop, in the full lustre of his Deportment.

He was a fat old gentleman with a false complexion, false teeth, false whiskers, and a wig. He had a fur collar, and he had a padded breast to his coat, which only wanted a star or a broad blue ribbon to be complete. He was pinched in, and swelled out, and got up, and strapped down, as much as he could possibly bear. He had such a neckcloth on (puffing his very eyes out of their natural shape), and his chin and even his ears so sunk into it, that it seemed as though he must inevitably double up, if it were cast loose. He had, under his arm, a hat of great size and weight, shelving downward from the crown to the brim; and in his hand a pair of white gloves, with which he flapped it, as he stood poised on one leg, in a high-shouldered, round-elbowed state of elegance not to be surpassed. He had a cane, he had an eye-glass, he had a snuff-box, he had rings, he had wristbands, he had everything but any touch of nature; he was not like youth, he was not like age, he was not like anything else in the world but a model of Deportment.

'Father! A visitor. Miss Jellyby's friend, Miss Summerson.'

'Distinguished,' said Mr Turveydrop, 'by Miss Summerson's presence.' As he bowed to me in that tight state, I almost believe I saw creases come into the whites of his eyes.

'My father,' said the son, aside to me, with quite an affecting belief in him, 'is a celebrated character. My father is greatly admired.'

'Go on, Prince! Go on!' said Mr Turveydrop, standing with his back to the fire, and waving his gloves condescendingly. 'Go on, my son!'

At this command, or by this gracious permission, the lesson went on. Prince Turveydrop sometimes played the kit, dancing; sometimes played the piano, standing; sometimes hummed the tune with what little breath he could spare, while he set a pupil right; always conscientiously moved with the least proficient through every step and every part of the figure; and never rested for an instant. His distinguished father did nothing whatever, but stand before the fire, a model of Deportment.

'And he never does anything else,' said the old lady of the censorious countenance. 'Yet would you believe that it's *his* name on the door-plate?'

'His son's name is the same, you know,' said I.

'He wouldn't let his son have any name, if he could take it from him,' returned the old lady. 'Look at the son's dress!' It certainly was plain – threadbare – almost shabby. 'Yet the father must be garnished and tricked out,' said the old lady, 'because of his Deportment. I'd deport him! Transport him would be better!'

I felt curious to know more concerning this person. I asked. 'Does he give lessons in Deportment, now?'

'Now!' returned the old lady, shortly. 'Never did.'

After a moment's consideration, I suggested that perhaps fencing had been his accomplishment?

'I don't believe he can fence at all, ma'am,' said the old lady.

I looked surprised and inquisitive. The old lady, becoming more and more incensed against the Master of Deportment as she dwelt upon the subject, gave me some particulars of his career, with strong assurances that they were mildly stated.

He had married a meek little dancing-mistress, with a tolerable connexion (having never in his life before done anything but deport himself), and had worked her to death, or had, at the best, suffered her to work herself to death, to maintain him in those expenses which were indispensable to his position. At once to exhibit his Deportment to the best models, and to keep the best models constantly before himself, he had found it necessary to frequent all public places of fashionable and lounging resort; to be seen at Brighton and elsewhere at fashionable times; and to lead an idle life in the very best clothes. To enable him to do this, the affectionate little dancing-mistress had toiled and laboured, and would have toiled and laboured to that hour, if her strength had lasted so long. For the mainspring of the story was that, in spite of the man's absorbing selfishness, his wife (overpowered by his Deportment) had, to the last, believed in him, and had, on her death-bed, in the most moving terms, confided him to their son as one who had an inextinguishable claim upon him, and whom he could never regard with too much pride and deference. The son, inheriting his mother's belief, and having the Deportment always before him, had lived and grown in the same faith, and now, at thirty years of age, worked for his father twelve hours a-day, and looked up to him with veneration on the old imaginary pinnacle. ...

My eyes were yet wandering, from young Mr Turveydrop working so hard, to old Mr Turveydrop deporting himself so beautifully, when the latter came ambling up to me, and entered into conversation.

He asked me, first of all, whether I conferred a charm and a distinction on London by residing in it? I did not think it necessary to reply that I was perfectly aware I should not do that, in any case, but merely told him where I did reside.

'A lady so graceful and accomplished,' he said, kissing his right glove, and afterwards extending it towards the pupils, 'will look leniently on the deficiencies here. We do our best to polish – polish – polish!'

He sat down beside me; taking some pains to sit on the form, I thought, in imitation of the print of his illustrious model on the sofa. And really he did look very like it.

'To polish – polish – polish!' he repeated, taking a pinch of snuff and gently fluttering his fingers. 'But we are not – if I may say so, to one formed to be graceful both by Nature and Art'; and with the high-shouldered bow, which it seemed impossible for him to make without lifting up his eyebrows and shutting his eyes – 'we are not what we used to be in point of Deportment.'

'Are we not, sir?' said I.

'We have degenerated,' he returned, shaking his head, which he could do, to a very limited extent, in his cravat. 'A levelling age is not favourable to Deportment. It develops vulgarity. Perhaps I speak with some little partiality. It may not be for me to say that I have been called, for some years now, Gentleman Turveydrop; or that His Royal Highness the Prince Regent did me the honour to inquire, on my removing my hat as he drove out of the Pavilion at Brighton (that fine building), "Who is he? Who the Devil is he? Why don't I know him? Why hasn't he thirty thousand a year?" But these are little matters of anecdote – the general property, ma'am, – still repeated, occasionally, among the upper classes.'

'Indeed?' said I.

He replied with the high-shouldered bow. 'Where what is left among us of Deportment,' he added, 'still lingers, England – alas, my country! – has degenerated very much, and is degenerating every day. She has not many gentlemen left. We are few. I see nothing to succeed us, but a race of weavers.'

'One might hope that the race of gentlemen would be perpetuated here,' said I.

'You are very good,' he smiled, with the high-shouldered bow again. 'You flatter me. But, no – no! I have never been able to imbue my poor boy with that part of his art. Heaven forbid that I should disparage my dear child, but he has – no Deportment.'

Arthur Hugh Clough (1819–1861)

Arthur Hugh Clough, born in the same year as Queen Victoria, was the son of a Liverpool cotton merchant. His family emigrated to America, where Clough spent his early years. He was educated in England at Rugby, under its headmaster, Dr Arnold, where he became a friend of Arnold's son, Matthew, the poet and critic. Dr Arnold placed a strong emphasis on developing personal discipline, both physical and moral, in his pupils, and encouraged qualities of leadership and fair-mindedness within a religious framework. His school was important in the development of the English public school system, which trained boys for their future roles as the administrators of Queen Victoria's steadily increasing British Empire.

Clough was head boy at Rugby, and won a scholarship to Balliol College, Oxford in 1836. Here he became involved in the religious debates of the time which were concerned with the identities of the Anglican and Roman Catholic churches and their relationship with the state. At first Clough was drawn towards Anglicanism, especially to the religious movement within the Church of England known as the Oxford Movement. Members of this group believed that the church was spiritually independent from the state, and that Anglicans should establish a middle ground between Roman Catholicism and Protestantism. Their beliefs later led some members of the Oxford Movement to join the Catholic church, while others remained as High Church Anglicans.

Clough became a Fellow of Oriel College, Oxford, but had to resign this position in 1848. Until 1871 it was essential for anyone appointed as a senior member of an Oxford college to accept in full the doctrines of the Church of England. These doctrines are stated in the Thirty Nine Articles, first agreed by bishops and archbishops in 1562, and still printed in the Book of Common Prayer. Because Clough had begun to suffer from serious religious doubts, he felt unable to do this, or to continue at Oxford. It may be difficult for some readers today to appreciate the importance of religious beliefs to many Victorians, and the pain which they suffered when new scientific and philosophical ideas caused them to doubt what they had previously believed.

Following his resignation from Oxford, Clough became principal of the student hostel at University College, London, which did not operate the same religious restrictions. He travelled to America, where he taught in Cambridge, Massachusetts, and became friendly with American intellectuals like Ralph Waldo Emerson (1803–1882) and Charles Eliot Norton (1827–1908). When he returned to England in 1853, he became Examiner in the Education Office. He wrote several long poems, in which he explored themes of self doubt and what he saw as the failings of Victorian society. His friend, Matthew Arnold, shared Clough's problems with religious doubt, and both men were concerned about what they saw as the decline of civilisation in the 19th century, as 'The Latest Decalogue' implies. Clough died of fever in Italy, and is buried in the Protestant cemetery in Florence. Matthew Arnold attributed his death at the relatively early age of 42 to 'premature despair'.

The most immediate context needed to appreciate the ironies in 'The Latest Decalogue' ('decalogue' means the Ten Commandments) is its intertextual references to those Commandments. The poem was first published in 1862, a year after his death, but the ideas in it were anticipated in a letter of 1846, in which Clough wrote with characteristic irony:

The very Decalogue itself – Thou shalt not do murder, Thou shalt not steal – may pass into a very dubious 'Thou shalt not do murder without great provocation' and 'Thou shalt not steal except now and then'.

The Ten Commandments are:

1 Thou shalt have none other gods but me.
2 Thou shalt not make to thyself any graven image, nor the likeness of anything that is in heaven above, or in the earth beneath, or in the water under the earth. Thou shalt not bow down to them nor worship them: for I the Lord thy God am a jealous God and visit the sins of the fathers unto the third and fourth generation of them that hate me, and shew mercy unto thousands in them that love me, and keep my commandments.
3 Thou shalt not take the name of the Lord thy God in vain: for the Lord will not hold him guiltless that taketh his name in vain.
4 Remember that thou keep holy the Sabbath day. Six days shalt thou labour, and do all that thou hast to do; but the seventh day is the Sabbath of the Lord thy God. In it thou shalt do no manner of work, thou, and thy son, and thy daughter, thy man-servant and thy maid-servant, thy cattle and the stranger that is within thy gates. For in six days the Lord made heaven and earth, the sea and all that in them is, and rested the seventh day; wherefore the Lord blessed the seventh day, and hallowed it.
5 Honour thy father and thy mother, that thy days may be long in the land which the Lord thy God giveth thee.
6 Thou shalt do no murder.
7 Thou shalt not commit adultery.
8 Thou shalt not steal.
9 Thou shalt not bear false witness against thy neighbour.
10 Thou shalt not covet thy neighbour's house, thou shalt not covet thy neighbour's wife, nor his servant, nor his maid, nor his ox, nor his ass, nor anything that is his.

The verse form which Clough chose for his parody of the Commandments is the eight-syllable rhyming couplet, popular with some Augustan poets, and used by Swift in his 'On the Death of Dr Swift'. Clough's use of the semi-colon, and its position in the lines, emphasises the irony and gives a twist to each Commandment, adding to each an oblique criticism of the ways Clough saw his contemporaries interpreting and breaking the Commandments.

'The Latest Decalogue' (1862)

Thou shalt have one God only; who
Would be at the expense of two?
No graven images may be

Worshipped, except the currency:
Swear not at all; for, for thy curse
Thine enemy is none the worse:
At church on Sunday to attend
Will serve to keep the world thy friend:
Honour thy parents; that is, all
From whom advancement may befall;
Thou shalt not kill; but need'st not strive
Officiously to keep alive:
Do not adultery commit;
Advantage rarely comes of it:
Thou shalt not steal; an empty feat,
When it's so lucrative to cheat:
Bear not false witness; let the lie
Have time on its own wings to fly:
Thou shalt not covet, but tradition
Approves all forms of competition.

Mark Twain (1835–1910)

Mark Twain's real name was Samuel Clemens. He was brought up in Hannibal, Missouri, a small town on the banks of the Mississippi river, at a time when slavery was still legal in the Southern States of America. After the death of his father when he was 12, Twain was apprenticed to a printer, and as a young man he travelled across America working as a typesetter, and later as a journalist. He returned to the Mississippi, and between 1857 and the start of the American Civil war in 1861, he achieved a boyhood ambition by becoming a licensed river boat pilot. He took his pseudonym, Mark Twain, from the shouts of the boat men sounding the depth of the river, and began using it for his professional writing from about 1861. 'Mark twain' means 'about 12 feet deep'; possibly Twain chose it to imply a risky depth for a writer who wanted to satirise aspects of life in America, as well as being dangerous for the big paddle steamers on the Mississippi.

The Civil War closed the Mississippi to river traffic; after it ended in 1865, Twain rapidly became a successful and prolific writer of short stories, humorous sketches and novels, as well as travel writing and journalistic reportage. He was also a celebrated and popular lecturer in Europe and America. In 1870 he married Olivia Langdon, whose family were staunch supporters of the abolition of slavery. Although Twain made a good living from his writing, he also invested his money unwisely, and in 1894 he was declared bankrupt. Although he recovered from this, personal tragedies, including the deaths of his wife and two of his daughters, made him increasingly pessimistic as he grew older, and his writing became more harsh and critical, and less warm-hearted and humorous. He died in Redding, Connecticut, at the age of 75.

Mark Twain is best known as a comic writer. Two of his best-known books, often described as books for boys, are *The Adventures of Tom Sawyer* (1876) and *The Adventures of Huckleberry Finn* (1884–1885), both of which draw on his childhood in Hannibal. *Tom Sawyer* is an entertaining boys' adventure story; although *Huckleberry Finn* was started simply as a sequel, it developed into a much more profound novel which, as well as often being extremely funny, also explores moral issues concerning slavery and freedom, and what it means to be 'civilised'. Although there is great comedy and humour in this novel, it also contains much satirical comment on American life in the 19th century.

All the contexts outlined in the Introduction to this book (see pages 8–10) and the questions posed there are relevant to reading *Huckleberry Finn*. In terms of genre, although it is a recognisably in the long tradition of the picaresque novel, Twain also created something which was entirely new in its day, in his use of the **vernacular** language and dialects through which he tells the story. As far as the author and period are concerned, *Huckleberry Finn* has always been a controversial book (see pages 105–108): on the one hand, it is acknowledged as a great, and essentially American, novel; on the other, it has been condemned as 'trash' and racist. The historical context, particularly an understanding of the history of slavery in the Southern States, is important for an appreciation of the character of Jim and the dangers which he and Huck run, as well as the moral struggle which Huck undergoes to escape from his own upbringing and prejudices. The reader's response is also a crucial context to consider in relation to *Huckleberry Finn*. As can be seen from the quotations from critics in Part 4: Critical approaches on pages 107–108, and as new readers of the book will realise for themselves, this is a book which each person has to interpret individually, in the light of their own experiences, their ethnic background, and their feelings about the issues it raises and the language Twain uses.

This extract is taken from Chapter 19 of *The Adventures of Huckleberry Finn*, approximately half way through the novel. The story is set on the Mississippi river in the period before the Civil War. Twain tells the story in the voice and the words of Huck Finn, a poor white boy who rebels against the genteel and civilising influence of the Widow Douglas, who has been trying to treat him as her son. Huck is running away from her and from his drunken and violent father. On the river he meets up with Jim, a runaway slave. They escape on a raft, both in search of freedom, and have many dangerous and comic encounters with different groups of people, including the two conmen who are introduced here. A 'jour printer' was a printer hired a day (from the French *jour*) at a time to do small jobs.

From *The Adventures of Huckleberry Finn* (1884–1885)

One of these fellows was about seventy, or upwards, and had a bald head and very gray whiskers. He had an old battered-up slouch hat on, and a greasy blue woolen shirt, and ragged old blue jeans britches stuffed into his boot tops, and home-knit galluses – no, he only had one. He had an old long-tailed blue jeans coat with slick brass buttons, flung over his arm, and both of them had big fat ratty-looking carpet-bags.

The other fellow was about thirty and dressed about as ornery. After breakfast we all laid off and talked, and the first thing that come out was that these chaps didn't know one another.

"What got you into trouble?" says the baldhead to t'other chap.

"Well, I'd been selling an article to take the tartar off the teeth – and it does take it off, too, and generly the enamel along with it – but I staid about one night longer than I ought to, and was just in the act of sliding out when I ran across you on the trail this side of town, and you told me they were coming, and begged me to help you to get off. So I told you I was expecting trouble myself and would scatter out *with* you. That's the whole yarn – what's yourn?"

"Well, I'd been a-runnin' a little temperance revival thar, 'bout a week, and was the pet of the women-folks, big and little, for I was makin' it mighty warm for the rummies, I *tell* you, and takin' as much as five or six dollars a night – ten cents a head, children and niggers free – and business a growin' all the time; when somehow or another a little report got around, last night, that I had a way of puttin' in my time with a private jug, on the sly. A nigger rousted me out this mornin', and told me the people was getherin' on the quiet, with their dogs and horses, and they'd be along pretty soon and give me 'bout half an hour's start and then run me down, if they could; and if they got me they'd tar and feather me and ride me on a rail, sure. I didn't wait for no breakfast – I warn't hungry."

"Old man," says the young one, "I reckon we might double-team it together; what do you think?"

"I ain't undisposed. What's your line – mainly?"

"Jour printer, by trade; do a little in patent medicines; theatre-actor – tragedy, you know; take a turn at mesmerism and phrenology when there's a chance; teach singing-geography school for a change; sling a lecture, sometimes – oh, I do lots of things – most anything that comes handy, so it ain't work. What's your lay?"

"I've done considerable in the doctoring way in my time. Layin' on o' hands is my best holt – for cancer, and paralysis, and sich things; and I k'n tell a fortune pretty good, when I've got somebody along to find out the facts for me. Preachin's my line, too; and workin' camp-meetin's; and missionaryin around."

Nobody never said anything for a while; then the young man hove a sigh and says –

"Alas!"

"What're you alassin' about?" says the baldhead.

"To think I should have lived to be leading such a life, and be degraded down into such company." And he begun to wipe the corner of his eye with a rag.

"Dern your skin, ain't the company good enough for you?" says the baldhead, pretty pert and uppish.

"Yes, it *is* good enough for me; it's as good as I deserve; for who fetched me so low, when I was so high? I did myself. I don't blame *you*, gentlemen – far from it; I don't blame anybody. I deserve it all. Let the cold world do its worst; one thing I know – there's a grave somewhere for me. The world may go on just as its always done, and take everything from me – loved ones, property, everything – but it can't take that. Some day I'll lie down in it and forget it all, and my poor broken heart will be at rest." He went on a-wiping.

"Drot your pore broken heart," says the baldhead; "what are you heaving your pore broken heart at *us* f'r? We hain't done nothing."

"No, I know you haven't. I ain't blaming you, gentlemen. I brought myself down – yes, I did it myself. It's right I should suffer – perfectly right – I don't make any moan."

"Brought you down from whar? Whar was you brought down from?"

"Ah, you would not believe me; the world never believes – let it pass – 'tis no matter. The secret of my birth -"

"The secret of your birth? Do you mean to say -"

"Gentlemen," says the young man, very solemn, "I will reveal it to you, for I feel I may have confidence in you. By rights I am a duke!"

Jim's eyes bugged out when he heard that; and I reckon mine did too. Then the baldhead says: "No! you can't mean it?"

"Yes. My great-grandfather, eldest son of the Duke of Bridgewater, fled to this country about the end of the last century, to breathe the pure air of freedom; married here, and died, leaving a son, his own father dying about the same time. The second son of the late duke seized the title and estates – the infant real duke was ignored. I am the lineal descendant of that infant – I am the rightful Duke of Bridgewater; and here am I, forlorn, torn from my high estate, hunted of men, despised by the cold world, ragged, worn, heart-broken, and degraded to the companionship of felons on a raft!"

Jim pitied him ever so much, and so did I. We tried to comfort him, but he said it warn't much use, he couldn't be comforted; said if we was a mind to acknowledge him, that would do him more good than most anything else; so we said we would, if he would tell us how. He said we ought to bow, when we spoke to him, and say 'Your Grace', or 'My Lord', or 'Your Lordship' – and he wouldn't mind it if we called him plain 'Bridgewater', which he said was a title, anyway, and not a name; and one of us ought to wait on him at dinner, and do any little thing for him he wanted done.

Well, that was all easy, so we done it. All through dinner Jim stood around and waited on him, and says, "Will yo' Grace have some o' dis, or some o' dat?" and so on, and a body could see it was mighty pleasing to him.

But the old man got pretty silent, by-and-by – didn't have much to say, and didn't look pretty comfortable over all that petting that was going on around that duke. He seemed to have something on his mind. So, along in the afternoon, he says:

"Looky here, Bilgewater," he says, "I'm nation sorry for you, but you ain't the only person that's had troubles like that."

"No?"

"No, you ain't. You ain't the only person that's been snaked down wrongfully out'n a high place."

"Alas!"

"No, you ain't the only person that's had a secret of his birth." And by jings, *he* begins to cry.

"Hold! What do you mean?"

"Bilgewater, kin I trust you?" says the old man, still sort of sobbing.

"To the bitter death!" He took the old man by the hand and squeezed it, and says, "The secret of your being: speak!"

"Bilgewater, I am the late Dauphin!"

You bet you Jim and me stared, this time. Then the duke says:

"You are what?"

"Yes, my friend, it is too true – your eyes is lookin' at this very moment on the pore disappeared Dauphin, Looy the Seventeen, son of Looy the Sixteen and Marry Antonette."

"You! At your age! No! You mean you're the late Charlemagne; you must be six or seven hundred years old, at the very least."

"Trouble has done it, Bilgewater, trouble has done it; trouble has brung these gray hairs and this premature balditude. Yes, gentlemen, you see before you, in blue jeans and misery, the wanderin', exiled, trampled-on and sufferin' rightful King of France."

Well, he cried and took on so, that me and Jim didn't know hardly what to do, we was so sorry – and so glad and proud we'd got him with us, too. So we set in, like we done before with the duke, and tried to comfort *him*. But he said it warn't no use, nothing but to be dead and done with it all could do him any good; though he said it often made him feel easier and better for a while if people treated him according to his rights, and got done on one knee to speak to him, and always called him 'Your Majesty', and waited on him first at meals, and didn't set down in his presence till he asked them. So Jim and me set to majestying him, and doing this and that and t'other for him, and standing up till he told us we might set down. This done him heaps of good, and so he got cheerful and comfortable. But the duke kind of soured on him, and didn't look a bit satisfied with the way things was going; still, the king acted real friendly towards him, and said the duke's great-grandfather and all the other Dukes of Bilgewater was a good deal thought of by his father and was allowed to come to the palace considerable; but the duke staid huffy a good while, till by-and-by the king says:

"Like as not we got to be together a blamed long time, on this h-yer raft, Bilgewater, and so what's the use o' your bein' sour? It'll only make things oncomfortable. It ain't my fault I warn't born a duke, it ain't your fault you warn't born a king – so what's the use to worry? Make the best o' things the way you find 'em, says I – that's my motto. This ain't no bad thing that we've struck here – plenty grub and an easy life – come, give us your hand, Duke, and less all be friends."

The duke done it, and Jim and me was pretty glad to see it. It took away all the uncomfortableness, and we felt mighty good over it, because it would a been a miserable business to have any unfriendliness on the raft; for what you want, above all things, on a raft, is for everybody to be satisfied, and feel right and kind towards the others.

It didn't take me long to make up my mind that these liars warn't no kings nor dukes, at all, but just low-down humbugs and frauds. But I never said nothing, never let on; kept it to myself; it's the best way; then you don't have no quarrels, and don't get into no trouble. If they wanted us to call them kings and dukes, I hadn't no objections, 'long as it would keep peace in the family; and it warn't no use to tell Jim, so I didn't tell him. If I never learnt anything else out of pap, I learnt that the best way to get along with his kind of people is to let them have their own way.

E. E. Cummings (1894–1962)

The poet who became E. E. Cummings was born Edward Estlin Cummings in Cambridge, Massachusetts, in 1894. His father was at the time a professor at Harvard, but then became a Unitarian minister. The house was full of books and Cummings' father loved word play, his sermons being full of puns and games with proverbs, mottoes and linguistic surprises. His mother, too, was literary, bringing her son up on a diet of poetry, particularly on the many occasions during his childhood when he was unable to attend school because of ill health.

Cummings began to write poetry early and had poems published before he entered Harvard, but he was a painter as well as a poet, always carrying a sketch book with him. He said, 'in the beginning was the Eye, not the Mind'. Richard S. Kennedy, in his biography of Cummings, *Dreams in the Mirror*, identifies seven values which were most important to Cummings: experience, creativity, uniqueness, primitiveness, freedom, independence and recognition of reality. At the same time, Cummings was lively company: Slater Brown, Cummings' companion in the ambulance corps in the First World War and later his room mate in New York recalled 'He was the most entertaining man I ever met ... He was a dreadful show-off. Everything he did was performance.'

Although Cummings' earliest poems are Keatsian in style, he soon cast aside more conventional forms, rebelling against realism. In his view

> ... the Symbol of all Art is the prism. The goal is unrealism. The method is destructive. To break up the white light of objective realism, into the secret glories which it contains.

He was influenced by jazz, and was technically very inventive. He experimented with making the appearance of the poem on the page, the lack of conventional punctuation and capital letters, and the visual effects of the layout and type face used, all contribute to its levels of meaning and mood.

Cummings presents his characters through voice. There are many individual voices in his work and he favoured phonetic reproduction of the spoken language, a device which Carol Ann Duffy also uses in her work. Like Duffy, too, Cummings used a lot of slang and unconventional written forms, to characterise types such as the 'redneck'.

As well as parodies of the politician and satire of traditional forms of expression, particularly poetic expression, Cummings often presents without comment opinions which he wants the reader to recognise as unacceptable in poems such as 'ygUDuh'. By the time he came to write this poem, the physical pain which he suffered throughout his life had become particularly severe; in order to cope with osteoarthritis in his spine he had to wear a specially designed corset. Some have linked this with the irritable growlings he expresses in his poems about social issues, domestic politics and the course of the war, growlings which became increasingly ill-tempered. Cummings was particularly troubled about the hatred engendered against the Japanese after America had joined the Second World War in 1941, the year 'ygUDuh' dates from. The poem is a carefully patterned satire against the inarticulate utterances of rage inspired by racism.

Those few critics who have written about Cummings have tended to concentrate on two contexts: the biographical and the linguistic. However, social and political contexts are also significant in his work.

"next to of course god america i
"next to of course god america i
love you land of the pilgrims' and so forth oh
say can you see by the dawn's early my
country 'tis of centuries come and go
and are no more what of it we should worry
in every language even deafanddumb
thy sons acclaim your glorious name by gorry
by jingo by gee by gosh by gum
why talk of beauty what could be more beautiful than these heroic happy dead
who rushed like lions to the roaring slaughter
they did not stop to think they died instead
then shall the voice of liberty be mute?"

He spoke.   And drank rapidly a glass of water

a salesman is an it that stinks Excuse
a salesman is an it that stinks Excuse

Me whether it's president of the you were say
or a jennelman name misder finger isn't
important whether it's millions of other punks
or just a handful absolutely doesn't
matter and whether it's in lonjewray

or shrouds is immaterial it stinks

a salesman is an it that stinks to please

but whether to please itself or someone else
makes no more difference than if it sells
hate condoms education snakeoil vac
uumcleaners terror strawberries democ
ra(caveat emptor)cy superfluous hair

or Think We've Met subhuman rights Before

ygUDuh
ygUDuh

       ydoan
       yunnuhstan

       ydoan o
       yunnuhstan dem
       yguduh ged

       yunnuhstan dem doidee
       yguduh ged riduh
       ydoan o nudn
LISN bud LISN
           dem
           gud
           am

           lidl yelluh bas
           tuds weer goin
duhSIVILEYEzum

Evelyn Waugh (1903–1966)

Arthur Evelyn St John Waugh was born in West Hampstead, London in 1903. His father was Arthur Waugh, a writer and publisher, and his elder brother, Alec, was also a writer, becoming a best-selling novelist while he was still in his late teens and therefore an even greater threat to Evelyn than his father. Much of Waugh's early life as a writer was spent trying to separate himself from both his father and his brother, and some of his earliest writings appeared to be partly satirical portraits of his brother and his experiences. It seems to have been very important to him to try to make his own mark as a writer quite distinct from his father and brother.

As fitted one of his class and upbringing he went to private preparatory school and then to Lancing, on the Sussex Downs, a school his father selected for him because from an early age Waugh showed great interest in religion. Lancing was a school well known for its High Anglicanism. From Lancing, he won a scholarship to Hertford College, Oxford, but he did little academic work and eventually ended up with a third class degree. In fact, he never graduated because in order to do so he would have to have studied for nine terms and he had only been at Oxford for eight. After his poor examination result his father was not willing to pay for the extra term which would have allowed him to receive his degree. At Oxford Waugh gave up the study of Modern History, becoming more interested in journalism, writing, editing, drawing and engraving. His first book was on the artist Dante Gabriel Rossetti.

Waugh's *Decline and Fall* was the first time that he showed evidence of a comic imagination. It was his first novel, begun at just about the time that his book on Rossetti was completed, and published in 1928. It was loosely and ironically modelled on Edward Gibbon's *The Decline and Fall of the Roman Empire* (1776–1788), a text all students of Modern History would have been familiar with at Oxford, and it uses Gibbon's characteristic irony.

Decline and Fall, therefore, was written at the time when Waugh was just establishing himself as a writer. It draws on some of his experiences as a teacher, for brief periods and in various circumstances. 1928 was also the year of his marriage to Evelyn Gardner, a marriage that only lasted for 15 months. Waugh's conversion to Catholicism came shortly afterwards, in 1930.

Much of what has been written on Waugh hinges on two main issues: the influence of Catholicism on his writing and the extent to which his work can be seen as satirical (see pages 108 109). He came to renounce the works he had written before his conversion, including *Decline and Fall*. Waugh himself denied that his works were satirical:

> Satire is a matter of period. It flourishes in a stable society and presupposes homogeneous moral standards – the early Roman Empire and 18th-century Europe. It is aimed at inconstancy and hypocrisy. It exposes polite cruelty and folly by exaggerating them. It seeks to produce shame. All this has no place in the Century of the Common Man where vice no longer pays any lip service to virtue.
>
> (*Fanfare*, 1945)

How much you agree with Waugh remains to be seen at the end of your study of satire.

The extract from *Decline and Fall* which follows comes from the early part of the novel when the main character, Paul Pennyfeather (whom Waugh did not describe as a hero because he said there were no heroes in the novel), is applying for a teaching job. Paul, an innocent and hardworking middle class student of theology, has been expelled from Oxford for indecent behaviour, having been caught up in the drunken horseplay of the aristocratic members of the Bollinger Club, debagged and forced to run the length of the college quadrangle without his trousers.

From *Decline and Fall* (1928)

'Sent down for indecent behaviour, eh?' said Mr Levy, of Church and Gargoyle, scholastic agents. 'Well, I don't think we'll say anything about that. In fact, officially, mind, you haven't told me. We call that sort of thing "Education discontinued for personal reasons," you understand.' He picked up the telephone. 'Mr Samson, have we any "education discontinued" posts, male, on hand?...Right!...Bring it up, will you? I think,' he added, turning again to Paul, 'we have just the thing for you.'

A young man brought in a slip of paper.

'What about that?'

Paul read it:

Private and Confidential Notice of Vacancy.

Augustus Fagan, Esquire, Ph.D., Llanabba Castle, N.Wales, requires immediately Junior assistant master to teach Classics and English to University Standard with subsidiary Mathematics, German, and French. Experience essential; first-class games essential.

Status of School: *School*

Salary offered: *£120 resident post.*

Reply promptly but carefully to Dr Fagan ('Esq., Ph.D.,' on envelope), enclosing copies of testimonials and photograph, if considered advisable, mentioning that you have heard of the vacancy through us.

'Might have been made for you,' said Mr Levy.

'But I don't know a word of German, I've had no experience, I've got no testimonials, and I can't play cricket.'

'It doesn't do to be too modest,' said Mr Levy. 'It's wonderful what one can teach when one tries. Why, only last term we sent a man who had never been in a laboratory in his life as senior Science Master to one of our leading public schools. He came wanting to do private coaching in music. He's doing very well, I believe. Besides, Dr Fagan can't expect all that for the salary he's offering. Between ourselves, Llanabba hasn't a good name in the profession. We class schools, you see, into four grades: Leading School, First-rate School, Good School, and School. Frankly,' said Mr Levy, 'School is pretty bad. I think you'll find it a very suitable post. So far as I know, there are only two other candidates, and one of them is totally deaf, poor fellow.'

Joseph Heller (1923–1999)

Joseph Heller was born in Brooklyn in 1923, the son of immigrant Russian parents. His father died when Joseph was four, leaving his mother, Lena, who spoke very little English, to bring him up along with the two children of his father's first marriage. Because of the poverty of his family, he left High School at 18 and worked in a variety of jobs until he completed his career as a bombardier and flew combat missions over Italy and France in the last two years of the Second World War. He was later to say:

> I am one of those who benefited from war. If I had not gone to war, I would not have gone to college, and if I had not gone to college, I would not have been a writer. I don't know what would have become of me.

Heller studied at New York University after the war, then at Oxford and eventually became a full-time advertising copywriter. He said when asked about whether being a novelist helped him to teach creative writing, that it rarely did – what helped most was the discipline learned as a copywriter.

He spent seven years writing his first novel, *Catch-22*, revising detail and structure carefully in order to make sure that the opening few chapters were sufficiently disordered in their sequence to allow the reader to experience the confusion of being involved in a war. When asked in 1975 in an interview for *Playboy* magazine how much material he had cut from *Catch-22* , Heller said:

> ... About 100 (pages).
> Playboy: What kind of material was it?
> Heller: Adjectives and adverbs.

Although he drew substantially on his own experiences of being in the Second World War, he was also fully aware that *Catch-22*, first published in 1961, also had much to say about other wars, in particular the Vietnam War.

The reception of the novel was mixed. Although large advertisements were placed in the influential papers, the response of reviewers varied from those who thought it one of the major works of the century to those who thought it had been thrown carelessly together. It never became a bestseller in the United States, although it topped the bestseller lists in Britain very soon after its publication there, and it has continued to sell large numbers of copies ever since, exceeding eight million copies sold by the mid 1970s.

Its genre has attracted a great deal of discussion. It is 'a moral book' according to Heller, 'dealing with man's moral dilemma. People can't distinguish between rational and irrational behaviour, between the moral and the immoral.' When asked whether he could himself make the distinction, he said 'I can, really. But it's not that easy. It's insane when I think this is a world in which the keepers are as nutty as the insane.'

Heller worked slowly and carefully on *Catch-22*, as he did on all his novels. Because the novel had so many characters in it, he kept a running chart showing who was involved with what and whom, and he decided on the ending long before he wrote the middle of the book:

> I suppose right after I sold the book, I was riding the subway one day, and I actually wrote the words to the ending – this was perhaps four years before the book was finished – and I didn't change it once. I couldn't see any alternative ending. It had a certain amount of integrity – not merely with the action of the book – that could've permitted anything – but the moral viewpoint in the book; the heavy suffusion of moral content which is in there, it seemed to me, required a resolution of choice rather than action.

The main character in the novel, Yossarian, is deliberately a cultural outsider. He is an Assyrian. Heller explained he had chosen this:

> Because I was looking for two things. I got the idea, frankly, from James Joyce's placing Bloom in Dublin. I wanted somebody who would be outside the culture in every way – ethically as well as others.
>
> Now, because America is a melting pot, there are huge concentrations of just about every other kind of nationality. I didn't want to give him a Jewish name, I didn't want to give him an Irish name, I didn't want to symbolise the white Protestant – but somebody who was almost a new man, and I made him Assyrian (but what I was ignorant of, for one thing, his name is not Assyrian; I've since been told it's Armenian).
>
> But I wanted to get an extinct culture, somebody who could not be identified with either geographically, or culturally, or sociologically – somebody as a person who has the capability of ultimately divorcing himself completely from all emotional and psychological ties.
>
> (Interview with Paul Krassner, 1962)

The extract which follows is perhaps the most famous part of the novel. It comes near the beginning where Yossarian speaks of the 'Catch-22' of the title, a phrase which has come to have universal relevance in the English language.

From *Catch-22* (1961)

It was a horrible joke, but Doc Daneeka didn't laugh until Yossarian came to him one mission later and pleaded again, without any real expectation of success, to be grounded. Doc Daneeka snickered once and was soon immersed in problems of his own, which included Chief White Halfoat, who had been challenging him all that morning to Indian wrestle, and Yossarian, who decided right then and there to go crazy.

"You're wasting your time," Doc Daneeka was forced to tell him.

"Can't you ground someone who's crazy?"

"Oh, sure. I have to. There's a rule saying I have to ground anyone who's crazy."

"Then why don't you ground me? I'm crazy. Ask Clevinger."

"Clevinger? Where is Clevinger? You find Clevinger and I'll ask him."

"Then ask any of the others. They'll tell you how crazy I am."

"They're crazy."

"Then why don't you ground them?"

"Why don't they ask me to ground them?"

"Because they're crazy, that's why."

"Of course they're crazy," Doc Daneeka replied. "I just told you they're crazy, didn't I? And you can't let crazy people decide whether you're crazy or not, can you?"

Yossarian looked at him soberly and tried another approach. "Is Orr crazy?"

"He sure is," Doc Daneeka said.

"Can you ground him?"

"I sure can. But first he has to ask me to. That's part of the rule."

"Then why doesn't he ask you to?"

"Because he's crazy," Doc Daneeka said. "He has to be crazy to keep flying combat missions after all the close calls he's had. Sure, I can ground Orr. But first he has to ask me to."

"That's all he has to do to be grounded?"

"That's all. Let him ask me."

"And then you can ground him?" Yossarian asked.

"No. Then I can't ground him."

"You mean there's a catch?"

"Sure there's a catch," Doc Daneeka replied. "Catch-22. Anyone who wants to get out of combat duty isn't really crazy."

There was only one catch and that was Catch-22, which specified that a concern for one's own safety in the face of dangers that were real and immediate was the process of a rational mind. Orr was crazy and could be grounded. All he had to do was ask; and as soon as he did, he would no longer be crazy and would have to fly more missions. Orr would be crazy to fly more missions and sane if he didn't, but if he was sane he had to fly them. If he flew them he was crazy and didn't have to; but if he didn't want to he was sane and had to. Yossarian was moved very deeply by the absolute simplicity of this clause of Catch-22 and let out a respectful whistle.

"That's some catch, that Catch-22," he observed.

"It's the best there is," Doc Daneeka agreed.

Carol Ann Duffy

Carol Ann Duffy was born in Glasgow in 1955 into a working class Catholic family. She moved to Stafford when she was young and was educated at Liverpool University. She had already published poems by the time she completed her degree, and won the National Poetry Competition in 1983.

Duffy has always been interested in the power of language and has said, 'Poetry has truth because it is rooted in truth, not academia.' When she moved to Stafford, she found herself adjusting her speech in order to fit in. By the time she was a teenager, she said, 'Poetry was my first love', and it is her respect for, and interest in, language that drives her – it is 'an almost physical presence, exciting, sexy, frightening, surprising'. At the time when she first became interested in poetry, poetry was itself becoming more populist, so that 'kids would go to poetry readings the way they would go to pop concerts'.

Duffy's early poems were often in the form of dramatic monologues, poems which feature immigrant school children, the oppressed, unhappy wives, Holocaust victims, psychopaths, murderers. Her interest in people's social contexts is evident in her first two volumes. *Standing Female Nude* (1985) and *Selling Manhattan* (1987) were political, confronting what Duffy saw as the greed of Margaret Thatcher's Britain with its accompanying racism and sexism. When she wrote 'Poet for our Times' she was working in East London where she was running workshops in a comprehensive school. The material of that poem had more personal interest for her, too, because her brother was at that time working in London as news editor for *The Daily Mirror*, and was particularly interested in the changes which had taken place in the tabloid newspapers, especially those which had come about through the involvement in British newspapers of Rupert Murdoch and Robert Maxwell. Her most recent poems, published in *The World's Wife* (1999) are also dramatic monologues. In these poems Duffy presents the wives of famous men telling their side of the stories, and offers a feminist perspective on male history and biography.

There is a clear social and political contemporary context which underlies the poems included here. Duffy is writing consciously about events which had recently happened and is drawing on the material of politics reported by the newspapers. She is therefore satirising both the government and the newspapers themselves. From the perspective of a historical context, Duffy draws on many contemporary events, expecting the reader to identify aspects of the Conservative government of the late 1980s and to recognise features of the presentation of tabloid newspapers, as well as references to the world-wide languages of wealth and poverty.

Given the interest today in identifying the purpose and audience of writing, it is interesting that Duffy has said in interviews, 'I've got no concept of writing for myself or anyone else at all. I suppose I'm writing for language.'

Poet for Our Times

I write the headlines for a Daily Paper.
It's just a knack one's born with all-right-Squire.
You do not have to be an educator,
just bang the words down like they're screaming *Fire!*
CECIL-KEAYS ROW SHOCK TELLS EYETIE WAITER.
ENGLAND FAN CALLS WHINGEING FROG A LIAR.

Cheers. Thing is, you've got to grab attention
with just one phrase as punters rush on by.
I've made mistakes too numerous to mention,
so now we print the buggers inches high.
TOP MP PANTIE ROMP INCREASES TENSION.
RENT BOY: ROCK STAR PAID ME WELL TO LIE.

I like to think that I'm a sort of poet
for our times. My shout. Know what I mean?
I've got a special talent and I show it
in punchy haikus featuring the Queen.
DIPLOMAT IN BED WITH SERBO-CROAT.
EASTENDERS' BONKING SHOCK IS WELL-OBSCENE.

Of course, these days, there's not the sense of panic
you got a few years back. What with the box
et cet. I wish I'd been around when the Titanic
sank. To headline that, mate, would've been the tops.
SEE PAGE 3 TODAY GENTS THEY'RE GIGANTIC.
KINNOCK-BASHER MAGGIE PULLS OUT STOPS.

And, yes, I have a dream – make that a scotch, ta –
that kids will know my headlines off by heart.
IMMIGRANTS FLOOD IN CLAIMS HEATHROW WATCHER.
GREEN PARTY WOMAN IS A NIGHTCLUB TART.
The poems of the decade ... *Stuff 'em! Gotcha!*
The instant tits and bottom line of art.

Making Money

Turnover. Profit. Readies. Cash. Loot. Dough. Income.
  Stash.
Dosh. Bread. Finance. Brass. I give my tongue over
to money; the taste of warm rust in a chipped mug
of tap-water. Drink some yourself. Consider
an Indian man in Delhi, Salaamat the *niyariwallah*,
who squats by an open drain for hours, sifting shit
for the price of a chapati. More than that. His hands
in crumbling gloves of crap pray at the drains
for the pearls in slime his grandfather swore he found.

Megabucks. Wages. Interest. Wealth. I sniff and snuffle
for a whiff of pelf; the stench of an abattoir blown
by a stale wind over the fields. Roll up a fiver,
snort. Meet Kim. Kim will give you the works,
her own worst enema, suck you, lick you, squeal
red weals to your whip, be nun, nurse, nanny,
nymph on a credit card. Don't worry.
Kim's only in it for the money. Lucre. Tin. Dibs.

I put my ear to brass lips; a small fire's whisper
close to a forest. Listen. His cellular telephone
rings in the Bull's car. Golden hello. Big deal. Now get
  this
straight. *Making a living is making a killing these days.*
Jobbers and brokers buzz. He paints out a landscape
by number. The Bull. Seriously rich. Nasty. One of us.

Salary. Boodle. Oof. Blunt. Shekels. Lolly. Gelt. Funds.
I wallow in coin, naked; the scary caress of a fake hand
on my flesh. Get stuck in. Bergama. The boys from the
  bazaar

hide on the target-range, watching the soldiers fire.
   Between bursts,
they rush for the spent shells, cart them away for scrap.
Here is the catch. Some shells don't explode. Ahmat
runs over grass, lucky for six months, so far. So
bomb-collectors die young. But the money's good.

Palmgrease. Smackers. Greenbacks. Wads. I widen my
   eyes
at a fortune; a set of knives on black cloth, shining,
utterly beautiful. Weep. The economy booms
like cannon, far out at sea on a lone ship. We leave
our places of work, tired, in the shortening hours, in
   the time
of night our town could be anywhere, and some of us
   pause
in the square, where a clown makes money swallowing
   fire.

Steve Bell

Steve Bell is one of England's leading political cartoonists. The main contexts of 'Righty Ho!' are historical, political and cultural. It was commissioned by the English and Media Centre in London in 1993: a Conservative government was in power, John Major was Prime Minister and John Patten Secretary of State for Education. National Curriculum tests in English were being developed for the first time. Many English teachers were opposed to testing 14-year-old students' knowledge and understanding of Shakespeare through an external examination then, and many still are. By referring ironically to both high and popular culture in its use of Shakespeare and Superman, Bell's cartoon still makes many relevant satirical points. Shakespeare is the icon of England and Englishness, and holds a central position in the education system as the representative of heritage and literary value. Bell's technique as a cartoonist also involves the use of consistent visual images to identify key figures: John Major, generally seen as a 'grey man', lacking in dynamism compared with his predecessor, Margaret Thatcher, is always shown by Bell wearing his underpants over his trousers. This is an ironic allusion to his lack of Superman's leadership qualities. Major and Patten have not stood the test of time, and focus groups have taken over from think tanks, but Bell's vision has proved prophetic. At the start of the new millennium, *Macbeth* has indeed replaced *Romeo and Juliet, A Midsummer Night's Dream* and *Julius Caesar* as a compulsory play in the tests for 14-year-olds in England!

4 | Critical approaches

- What does the word 'reading' mean?

- How important are both the writer and the reader in relation to a text?

- How have critical approaches changed during the 20th century?

- How does knowing about critical approaches to satirical texts help a reader to understand a text better?

What does the word 'reading' mean?

In the context of studying literature 'reading' means more than just being able to decipher the symbols on a printed page. It means more than being able to take in the information on the page. Reading is about making sense of what is read, about seeing how texts have been put together, and why writers have done it in a particular way, and why they have chosen to use certain kinds of language to express their ideas and feelings. Reading literature is an active process for the reader.

The writer and the text

Clearly the writer is the person who made all the choices while writing the text. Different theoretical schools of thought, however, have had very different ideas about the significance of the writer once the work has been completed and published. At one extreme is the 'intentionalist' position, which says that what a writer intended (the authorial intention) is the most important thing in interpreting the text. Complications arise here when a distinction is made between the writer's conscious and unconscious choices. At the other end of the spectrum is '**reader response theory**', the school of thought which says that once the work is completed, then it is entirely independent of its creator and it is the reader who is the important factor. There are, though, other positions which can be held. Some critics favour interpreting the text through what they know about the writer's background and life. Others favour interpreting the text through the filter of all the other works a writer has produced, a position most easily held when the writer is dead and when all his or her work can be considered. A particular text, therefore, can be positioned with regard to that writer's complete works, or **oeuvre**.

The reader and the text

In the early 1990s the German poet and critic, Hans Magnus Enzenburger, painted this exhilarating picture of what it is to be a reader:

The reader is always right, and no-one can take away the freedom to make whatever use of a text which suits him. ... This freedom also includes the right to leaf backwards and forwards, to skip whole passages, to read sentences against the grain, to misunderstand them, to spin sentences out and embroider them with every possible association, to draw conclusions from the text, of which the text knows nothing, to be annoyed at it, to be happy because of it, to forget it, to plagiarise it and to throw the book in which it is printed into the corner at any time he likes.

Studying a literary text is an interaction between the reader and the text, which is not going to result in final 'right' answers. It is the reader's job to respond, to think, to engage with and to interpret what he or she reads – to make meanings from the text, based on evidence from within and around it. Because of differences between people in their experiences, education, gender, ethnicity and class, no-one interprets a text in exactly the same way as anyone else. Thus, there can be alternative ways of reading the same texts by different people, or by the same reader revisiting the text at different times.

Andrew Hoffman, writing in 1988 about Mark Twain and his work, comments on the relationship of the reader with a text, the usefulness of historical or biographical contexts, and the importance of the reader in keeping a text alive:

We read from a time, not of a time. Using a novel to understand history must of necessity produce as many difficulties as using history to understand a novel, looking at a piece of fiction as a sort of expression of the age in which it is written. We are hampered by distance: between our time and the author; between the author and the time he or she writes of, and between the author and his or her own time. Biographical criticism attempts to fill that last chasm, but its information and efforts can never equal the task. As Twain said to introduce his autobiography, what someone does comprises only a tiny fraction of a life; what passes through a mind makes up most of it, and that can never be fully recorded ... When Mark Twain writes about the Mississippi valley before the Civil War, we construct our vision of the world he describes as much from the vision of that time and place that we have gained elsewhere as from Twain's own words. We read the book today. The book will be read tomorrow only if it has meaning for tomorrow's readers.

(Andrew Jay Hoffman *Twain's Heroes; Twain's Worlds*, 1988)

▶ How easily could you adapt Hoffman's comments about *Huckleberry Finn* to any other satirical text or texts you have studied?

Critical approaches in the 20th century

During the 20th century literary theory has become an area of study in its own right, especially at university level. It draws on a wide range of interdisciplinary studies – linguistics, history, psychology, women's studies and cultural studies, for example – and generates its own debates and discussions, arguments and counter arguments among critics. Critical approaches derive from these theories and are about different ways of reading texts – they have a history, in the same way that literature has. New approaches develop out of, or in reaction to, older ones.

Just as it may be helpful to see the contexts of a text as keys to unlocking its meaning, it may be helpful to see critical approaches as tools to use when reading. They take as their main focus for reading and interpretation:

- the text itself

- the author of the text

- the reader's response to the text

- the context in which the text was written.

Within any of these, there are different ways of reading which readers can adopt. Put very simply:

a Marxist perspective might look particularly at power relationships, representations of different social groups, and the importance of property and money

a feminist perspective might consider the role of women in the text, and how they are presented

a psychoanalytic perspective might consider aspects of sexuality, and uses of imagery

a structuralist perspective might analyse how language is used to expose the ways in which the text is constructed

a new historicist perspective might look at the relationship between the text and the society within which it was produced.

These 'new' ways of reading developed during the second part of the 20th century in opposition to the 'traditional' critical approach which had become so well established in the study of English literature as to appear to be the correct way in which to study a literary text. This is the method derived from the work of I.A. Richards and F.R. Leavis in Cambridge during the first half of the 20th century, when English was being established as a discipline worthy of academic study at universities in its own right. Leavis and his contemporaries believed that:

- there are great works which everyone should study – the **canon**, or definitive list of the major classic texts, of English literature
- these great works of literature are timeless, and valuable because they are great works of art
- a text should be studied and judged objectively, through close reading of the text itself, without concern for information about the writer or context
- everybody has the capacity to be moved and improved by literature, provided they have sufficient sensitivity to it.

These views have had a powerful influence on English teaching, but recent critical approaches have all challenged them in one way or another, although none of them would question or abandon the need for close and careful reading. In his own writings, Leavis gives many examples of his own skills as a reader and interpreter, but he does also imply that there is a 'right' way to read a text. Look, for example, at his comments on Popes's satirical bias in his essay on Pope in *Revaluation: Tradition and Development in English Poetry*:

> It is, in some ways, a pity that we know so much about Pope's life. If nothing had been known but the works, would envy, venom, malice, spite, and the rest have played so large a part in the commentary? There is, indeed, evidence in the satires of strong personal feelings, but even – or rather, especially – where these appear strongest, what (if we are literate) we should find most striking is an intensity of art.

In this essay, written in 1936, Leavis is doing a demolition job on contemporary critics who argued that Pope's expressions of personal spite and malice are explicable because he was disabled, and that readers enjoy reading them. Many of Leavis' assumptions as a critic are evident in the short extract above:

- He would prefer not to contextualise a text in a writer's biography. The text is the subject of study, and the trained reader can read and appreciate it without contextual clues.
- He has a particular co-reader in mind, someone who reads in the same ways as he does, who has had the same education in reading, and who has reached a certain standard of approaching and appreciating texts. This person will therefore be a 'literate' person. 'Literacy' at the beginning of the 21st century is more likely to mean equipping people with the basic skills they need to read the print around them in everyday life. For Leavis, the word 'literate' carries much more baggage in terms of education, social class, the kinds of texts read, and the response to them.

- He expects readers to agree with him. His use of 'we' implies a group of like-minded readers. It may feel inclusive for these people, but if a reader disagrees, or finds him or herself unable to see the same merits in a text as Leavis does, it excludes them. This leaves little room for alternative interpretations by readers who may come from a different educational background, social class, gender or race from Leavis.

- He knows how literature ought to affect readers, and how they ought to react – or thinks he does. Note the use of the word 'should', not 'may', 'might', or 'could'. There is an obligation on the reader to see the same merits in the text as he does.

Examinations in Literature all expect students to be able to read texts closely, and express their own opinions about them. The techniques of reading owe a great deal to Leavis and his followers. However, the current emphasis on expressing individual opinions, informed by other readers' interpretations, recognises that there are also many critical approaches which make different sets of assumptions about which texts are worth studying and how they are read and interpreted.

Critical approaches to some key satirical texts

Seeing how a text was received when it was first published and how attitudes to it have changed over time can be helpful in developing a fuller understanding of the text itself and confirming one's own reading of it. It is useful to consider what aspects of the text earlier critics have chosen to focus on, and what assumptions they are making about it – these judgements have a historical context just as the text has. The following selections of approaches to the work of some of the writers in Part 3 (Chaucer, Dryden, Jane Austen, Mark Twain and Evelyn Waugh) have been chosen to illustrate the different approaches of critics, either writing at the time of publication or as later readers. The assignments which follow in Part 5 provide opportunities to put into practice some of the critical approaches outlined in this Part.

Critics on Geoffrey Chaucer

Caxton was Chaucer's publisher, rather than a critic of his work. Writing in 1484, he recognised Chaucer's importance as the first poet to write in English (not Latin or French), and comments on his particular skills as a writer of prose and verse:

> In especial ... we ought to gyue a synguler laude vnto that noble and grete philosopher Gefferey Chaucer, the whiche for his ornate wrytyng in our tongue may wel haue the name of a laureate poete. For tofore that he by hys labour enbelysshyd, ornated and made faire our Englisshe ... he made many bokes and treatyces ... as wel in metre as in ryme and prose, and them so craftyly made that he

comprehended his maters in short, quyck, and hye sentences, eschewing prolyxyte, castyng away the chaff of superfluyte, and shewing the pyked grayn of sentence utteryd by crafty and sugred eloquence.

(William Caxton Proem to Caxton's second edition of *The Canterbury Tales*, 1484)

By 1700, people had begun to criticise Chaucer's poetry for being too 'rough' and full of 'mouldy words' (Samuel Cobb *Poetae Brittanica*, c 1700). In his Preface to a work which contains his translations of some of *The Canterbury Tales* into 'modern' English, Dryden focuses on Chaucer as a writer about life – a realist, who tells us the truth – and stresses the universality and permanence of his descriptions of people. Although he is writing as a translator of one kind of English into another, Dryden's attention has shifted from Chaucer's language to his subject matter and to the poems as documentary – a window into the life of the Middle Ages:

He must have been a man of a most wonderful comprehensive nature, because, as it has been truly observed of him, he has taken into the compass of his *Canterbury Tales* the various manners and humours (as we now call them) of the whole English nation, in his age ... We have our fore fathers and great grand-dames all before us, as they were in Chaucer's days; their general characters are still remaining in mankind, and even in England.

(John Dryden Preface to *Fables Ancient and Modern*, 1700)

In the 20th century, critical attention shifts again to focus on Chaucer the writer, not Chaucer the reporter, as these titles of essays in the Macmillan Casebook edited by J.J. Anderson (1974) show: 'The idiom of popular poetry in *The Miller's Tale*'; 'Irony in *The Wife of Bath's Tale*'; 'The narrative art of *The Pardoner's Tale*'.

Dr Johnson on John Dryden's *Absalom and Achitophel*

The extracts below about the satirical poem *Absalom and Achitophel* are all taken from Dr Johnson's essay on Dryden in *Lives of the Poets*, published 1779–1781, 70 years after Dryden's death. The essay is basically biographical. Johnson explains the popularity of the poem as a mixture of topicality and good writing which aroused strong feelings in readers. He is reading the poem in several different ways:

- when he considers the author's intention, he admires it as a piece of writing with a particular audience and purpose, written in an appropriate style
- when he considers it as a constructed text, he finds faults in its structure
- when he matches it against what he thinks poetry should be – something expressed

in beautiful language, with plenty of images and descriptions, and with subject matter that is 'clean' and expresses moral values which he agrees with – he does not approve of Dryden's poem.

In November 1681 Dryden became yet more conspicuous by uniting politics with poetry in the memorable satire called *Absalom and Achitophel*, written against the faction which, by Lord Salisbury's incitement, set the Duke of Monmouth at its head.

Of this poem, in which personal satire was applied to the support of public principles, and in which therefore every mind was interested, the reception was eager, and the sale large.

The reason of this general perusal Addison has attempted to derive from the delight which the mind feels in the investigation of secrets; and thinks that curiosity to decipher the names procured readers to the poem. There is no need to enquire why those verses were read, which, to all the attractions of wit, elegance, and harmony, added the co-operation of all the factious passions, and filled every mind with triumph or resentment. ...

If *Absalom and Achitophel* is to be considered as a poem political and controversial, it will be found to comprise all the excellences of which the subject is susceptible – acrimony of censure, elegance of praise, artful delineation of characters, variety and vigour of sentiment, happy turns of language, and pleasing harmony of numbers ...

It is not however without faults; some lines are inelegant or improper, and too many are irreligiously licentious. The original structure of the poem was defective; allegories drawn at great length will always break; Charles could not run continually parallel with David. The subject has likewise another inconvenience; it admitted little imagery or description ...

20th-century critics on Jane Austen's *Northanger Abbey*

Here are two 20th-century critics offering alternative ways of looking at the relationship of content and structure in *Northanger Abbey*. Marvin Mudrick (1952) argues that the parody of the plot and characters of the typical gothic novel is central to Jane Austen's novel, and enables her to comment ironically on gothic fiction and on real life. Elizabeth Hardwick (1965) has a quite different, more thematic reading of what the novel is about and how it is structured. These alternative readings are not incompatible – they are both ways of looking at structure, style and theme.

Northanger Abbey is as much domestic novel as parody. Irony overtly juxtaposes the Gothic and the bourgeois worlds, and allows them to comment on each other.

Instead of reproducing the Gothic types of character and situation, she presents their anti-types in the actual world, and organises these into a domestic narrative that parallels or intersects, and at all points is intended to invalidate, the Gothic narrative to which it diligently corresponds ... For all the malice, hypocrisy, treachery, and general wickedness at Udolpho, Jane Austen finds very satisfactory counterparts at Bath. What her irony does here is to diminish scale, to puncture the grandiose pretensions of the Gothic villains, to demonstrate what villainy is like when transferred to the everyday, middle class, social world.

(Marvin Mudrick 'Irony versus Gothicism' in *Jane Austen: Irony as Defence and Discovery*, 1952)

... the part of the novel designed to be satire on the extremely popular Gothic mysteries of the time is actually the merest side issue, not even a true subplot, and ... the weakest part of a strong novel.

[*Northanger Abbey*] is an engaging story of human beings in pursuit of love, money and pleasure ... this pursuit is not always light-hearted and innocently romantic. A good deal of cynicism accompanies the chase ... the plot, on the surface, seems amusing enough, but there is genuine cruelty in the working out of it.

Bath itself is almost the central character of the first part of the book, just as Northanger Abbey, and all it means, is at the centre of the second half of the novel. ... The plot of *Northanger Abbey* finally rests upon love of money, or perhaps we should use the stronger word, greed.

(Elizabeth Hardwick from the Afterword in the New English Library edition of *Northanger Abbey*, 1965)

Black and white critics on Mark Twain's *Huckleberry Finn*

A variety of different critical approaches is evident in responses to *The Adventures of Huckleberry Finn* since its publication in 1884. They focus on:

- the **canonical** status of the text – whether it does or does not deserve to be included in lists of great American literary texts

- readers' responses, especially those of black readers, to the controversial issues of language and the use of stereotypes in the novel

- debates about censorship and the function of literature in education

- discussion of the author's intentions

- close analysis of Twain's style, and uses of irony in his satirical text
- exploration of the structures and symbolism of the text.

The novel has always been controversial, but the arguments about it have shifted since it was first published from whether or not it is a moral book, to whether or not it is a racist book. Initially some readers found Huck's language and morals offensive. In 1885 it was banned from the shelves of the Public Library in Concord, Massachusetts. One of the Library Committee members said:

> It deals with a series of adventures of a very low grade of morality; it is couched in the language of a rough, ignorant dialect, and all through its pages there is a systematic use of bad grammar and an employment of rough, coarse, inelegant expressions. To sum up, the book is flippant and irreverent in its style. It deals with a series of experiences that are certainly not elevating. The whole book is of a class that is more profitable for the slums, than it is for respectable people, and it is trash of the veriest sort.

Twain's response to this in his autobiography focuses on a key point in the narrative, and on Huck's moral decision about his relationship with Jim:

> When Huck appeared, twenty one years ago, the public library of Concord flung him out indignantly, partly because, after deep mediation and careful deliberation he made up his mind on a difficult point, and said that if he'd got to betray Jim or go to hell, he would go to hell – which was profanity, and those Concord purists couldn't understand it.

The opinions of white writers and critics have all contributed to the book's status as one of the great American novels and one of the most frequently taught in American schools. T.S. Eliot, the poet and critic, said 'the character of Huckleberry Finn is one of the permanent symbolic figures of fiction'. Ernest Hemingway said:

> All modern American literature comes from one book by Mark Twain called *Huckleberry Finn* … It's the best book we've had. All American writing comes from that, there was nothing before. There has been nothing as good since.

But for black readers and critics, the text is much more problematic. After desegregation legislation in the Southern States of America in the 1950s, and the integration of schools, the focus of objections shifted to Twain's use of racist language, and his presentation of black people through the character of Jim, the runaway slave.

Thus, as well as being a frequently taught text, it is also one of those most frequently challenged as offensive by parents and school governors. For black readers, separating the text and the contexts in which it was written and in which it is now read is extremely difficult. The essays in *Satire or Evasion? Black Perspectives on Huckleberry Finn* (eds. James Leonard, Thomas Tenney, Thadious Davis, 1992) show critics arguing about whether or not it is a racist book, reading the same pieces of text closely, but arriving at very different – often opposite – interpretations of it. These arguments look hard at the historical context of the novel, Twain's use of language, his handling of dialogue, and his uses of stereotypes in presenting his characters. Many of the debates hinge on perceptions of Twain's use of irony and his intentions in writing the book, and on differing views about the effect of literature on readers, and its value to them.

The most vociferous opponent of teaching *Huckleberry Finn* in schools is John Wallace, who writes:

> *Huckleberry Finn* is an American classic for no other reason than that it ridicules blacks to a greater extent than any other book given to our children to read. The book and racism feed on each other and have withstood the test of time because many Americans insist on preserving our racist heritage.
>
> (John H. Wallace 'The case against Huck Finn')

Richard Barkdale answers back with a discussion of Twain's tone and authorial intention:

> By bringing black runaway Jim into close association with white runaway Huck, Twain obviously desired to explore the ironic implications of such an association in a 'sivilisation' riddled by racial division and prejudice ... Twain appears to be asking ... how truly civilised an America is which since its beginning has cultivated and nurtured slavery. He knew, as he observed events in the 1880s, that although slavery no longer officially existed, blacks were still ... exploited and kept illiterate, disenfranchised, and socially and culturally oppressed.
>
> Twain appears to suggest, with more than just an ironic gleam in his eye, that such a friendship (between Huck and Jim) could develop only on a socially isolated raft in the middle of the nation's biggest and longest river, and thus as far from the shores ruled by law and

order as a person could get in middle America.

The continuing controversy about *The Adventures of Huckleberry Finn* suggests that the American reading public, in the main, has never fully understood the writer's ironic message.

(Richard K. Barkdale 'History, slavery and thematic irony')

The other area for debate for black and white critics is the ending of the novel. Some see the last section, at the Phelps plantation, as a flaw in the overall structure of the text; others find thematic or structural justifications for it. In discussing Twain's presentation of Jim, Betty H. Jones defends Twain as a satirist, and also sees deeper patterns of symbolism underlying the narrative which explain the characterisation and also provide the novel's structure:

> The satirist enjoys the freedom to move his characters about at will, making them both targets of the satiric thrust and mouthpieces for the authorial voice. Characters may sometimes be victims and pawns; at other times they may be active agents. Ultimately, the satirist as social reformer will do with his characters whatever he needs to do to act as a corrective agent for the society he portrays.
>
> ... Jim's presence in *Huckleberry Finn* sets up mythic resonances that reverberate throughout the work ... part of Jim's real function (as Huck's wise mentor and spiritual father) is to contribute to and extend the mythic-archetypal patterns that operate just beneath the surface of Twain's text. ... the picaresque structure of Twain's novel accommodates itself to the series of journeys Huck must take, each bringing him closer to maturity ...
>
> (Betty H. Jones 'Huck and Jim: A reconsideration')

Warren Beck sees the novel as structured around a series of opposites:

> The pattern of the novel turns on an equilibrium of opposites; escape and confrontation, evasion and commitment and fantasy and reality, and thereby achieves its logical symmetry and aesthetic unity.
>
> (Warren Beck 'Huck Finn at Phelps farm – essay in defence of novel's form')

20th-century critics on Evelyn Waugh

Critics writing about Waugh's novels seem to spend a lot of their time arguing about whether or not he is a satirist, and whether or not the novels have deeper themes and significance than appear at first sight. Their arguments reinforce the definition of reading as interpretation, rather than just being a concern with the plot and the interaction of characters, even in apparently light and humorous satirical writing. Some of these more extreme ideas should also act as warnings to readers always to test a critic's opinons against their own knowledge and understanding of the text.

> The titles of Waugh's early satires – *Decline and Fall*, *Vile Bodies*, *A Handful of Dust* – are important keys to the seriousness of attitude which informs them. The decay of a civilisation, futile sensuality leading to boredom, the poverty of spiritual life – these are the subjects of the first three works.
>
> (James Carens *The Satiric Art of Evelyn Waugh*, 1966)

> To the satirist it is the object of his humour that matters, the point of view it serves; what matters to Waugh is the humour itself: it is vital only that the texture of life should be made to yield a comic response rather than a bitter or tragic one.
>
> (Ian Littlewood *Writings of Evelyn Waugh*, 1983)

> Waugh's early novels are surreal, fantasticated, and ostensibly amoral, but on the figurative level they are parables about freedom, servitude and vocation.
>
> (Jeffrey Heath *The Picturesque Prison: Evelyn Waugh and his Writing*, 1982)

> Waugh's novels are not primarily interesting for their spiritual content, or moral theology, or satiric themes, or realistic presentation of life; their power resides in their creation of a living fictional world, a caricature that reveals elemental mythic patterns and tensions beneath the random, cluttered surface of life.
>
> (Robert R. Garnett *From Grimes to Brideshead – the early novels of Evelyn Waugh*, 1990)

> Symbols are always the key to Waugh's art ... Paul's circular experience ... can be seen as a modern parody of the fruitful cycle of the seasons and the sacred cycle of the Christian calendar, models that expose the futility of the contemporary secular world. Paul is the parodic Christ ...
>
> (Jerome Meckier 'Circle, symbol and parody in Evelyn Waugh's *Decline and Fall*' 1979)

1 Select any one writer from the 'golden age' of satire. Look up the entries for him or her in reference books such as the *Dictionary of National Biography*, the *Oxford Companion to English Literature* and on internet websites. Compare the attitudes to your chosen writer and to satire as a mode of writing implied or explicitly stated in these entries.

2 Choose one of the authors whose work has been discussed in detail in Part 4. Which critical views about this writer do you find come closest to your own views, and why?

3 Richard Sheridan wrote a play, *The Critic* (1779), satirising the theatre of his day and the way critics could make or destroy a play's success. Examine some theatre or television reviews by today's reviewers: how easy would it be to satirise or parody their writing?

4 A burlesque is 'a literary composition or dramatic representation which aims at exciting laughter by the comical treatment of a serious subject or the caricature of the spirit of a serious work' *(Oxford Companion to English Literature)*. How useful is this critical term as a way of explaining the satirical method of any of the texts you have studied?

5 Choose two contrasting passages of criticism from Part 4. How far can they be subjected to the same kind of critical analysis that you would use for discussing the satirical texts themselves?

5 | How to write about satirical texts

'The profitable discussion of literature'

At the end of his Introduction to *Revaluation: Tradition and Development in English Poetry*, F.R. Leavis writes:

> I think it is the business of the critic to perceive for himself, to make the finest and sharpest relevant discriminations, and to state his findings as responsibly, clearly, and forcibly as possible. Then even if he is wrong he has forwarded the business of criticism – he has exposed himself as openly as possible to correction; for what criticism undertakes is the profitable discussion of literature.

It is not necessary to be a professional critic to take part in this 'profitable discussion' – every reader can do it. Look again at Part 1: Approaching the subject (pages 16–17) and the paragraphs there about the skills needed to read satire and to write about it; and at Part 2: Approaching the texts (pages 27–30) at the paragraphs on recognising a writer's attitude, tone and mood. In order to write effectively about it, the reader of satire needs to be alert to the surface and deeper meanings of the text – the ways in which the content reflects the writer's criticisms of people and society. For example, think about how Swift uses size in the first two Parts of *Gulliver's Travels* to highlight what he considers to be the trivial political preoccupations of 18th-century England, and also the small-minded, warmongering patriotism of Gulliver in contrast to the humane ideals of the King of Brobdingnag. The reader also needs to be sensitive to the wide range of tones which a satirist may adopt, and to the ways in which the writer's choices of language affect these.

Developing your own critical reading and writing

Here are some questions you can use in your own critical reading and writing, as tools to help you to focus on different aspects of any text, not just satirical ones, and to organise your responses to it. The groups of questions focus on the skills and understanding of texts that you need to develop in order to arrive at your own informed opinions about them, and that you should be able to demonstrate when talking or writing about them. These skills include:

- an overall grasp of the content of the text
- an understanding of the ways in which writers' choices of form, language and structure shape the meanings of a text

- an awareness of alternative ways of interpreting a text
- an awareness of the relevance of different kinds of knowledge about the contexts in which the text was produced and is read.

The groups of questions below are intended to be applicable to any literary text. To practise using them, choose one of the extracts in Part 3 which you have not already worked on in detail. Read it through several times and then make brief notes of your answers to each of the questions listed under these two headings: First impressions of the content and meaning, and Language, form, structure and genre. Doing this should give you some ways in to, and sufficient materials for, a critical commentary on a piece of literature which you have not previously studied.

When using the groups of questions on a text which you have been studying in detail, also use the questions listed under Biographical, historical and cultural contexts in order to consolidate what you have learned, and to help you evaluate the significance of relevant context to that particular text. Finally, use the last pair of questions to help you reflect on your own reading and to draw together your own ideas and opinions about it.

The example notes in brackets all refer to the extract from *Bleak House* on pages 72–75. Before working on a text of your own choice, read the passage several times and supplement the notes with examples and details from the text, and any further points you would want to make about it.

First impressions of the content and meaning

- What aspects of the text do you place emphasis on and why?

  (Presentation of Mr Turveydrop – he seems to be the centre of attention for the narrator and the characters.)

- Which parts of, or details from the text are you putting together to create your meanings?

  (Description of him, what the narrator say about him, what the old lady says, what Mr T says himself, how he behaves.)

- What do you think are the key ideas in the text?

  (The man's absorbing selfishness.)

- What is it that makes you think these are the key ideas?

  (The way the passage concentrates on him; his treatment of his son; picking up on other character's views about him.)

Language, form, structure and genre

- What aspects of the language are interesting?

  (Use of dialogue and different voices to reveal character; use of lists in descriptions; use of reported speech for old lady's account.)

- How do the sequence and structure of the text determine the way you respond to it?

  (Extract follows a realistic sequence of meeting someone for the first time and getting to know them; reader partners the narrator in developing judgements about Mr T.)

- What does the writer's choice of form and genre tell you about the text?

  (Prose; fiction; episode in a novel; could speculate on thematic content.)

- What models are helpful for you to draw on when thinking about this particular text (such as Marxist, feminist, psychoanalytic, structuralist, new historicist)?

  (Might use Marxist: Mr T's social class; attitudes to money; exploitation of his hard-working son; definitions of a 'gentleman'. Or might use feminist: Mr T seen through the eyes of Esther and the old lady; comparison of male and female points of view and moral attitudes. Or might use psychoanalytical: the parent–child relationship. Or new historicist: the Regency dandy as a type, using pictures to illuminate Dicken's satire.)

- What features of this text make you relate it, by comparison or contrast, to other texts that you know?

  (Relates to other novels by Dickens through uses of language, method of presenting character, narrative style. Contrast with other first-person narratives, e.g. *Catcher in the Rye*, *Huckleberry Finn*) where the authorial voice is not allowed to intrude as it does here.)

Biographical, historical and cultural contexts

- What knowledge about the writer helps you to understand more about the text?

  (Can see Dickens' sympathy with the underdog, and his antipathy to selfishness; possibly a reflection of his own unsatisfactory father.)

- What aspects of the period in which the text was written jump out at you as important or interesting?

  (A 19th-century novel, so the episode is developed at length, not compressed as it might be in a modern text; Mr T himself is a leftover from an earlier period in clothes and behaviour. He belongs to the Regency, not the mid-Victorian period when the text was written.)

- What evidence can you find in the text about the attitudes and values of the characters, or the writer?

  (All in the language: the writer makes it clear that the attitudes and values of Mr T and the narrator are in conflict. The reader is led to side with the narrator.)

- In what ways do you as a modern reader respond differently from the way you think a reader at the time the text was written would have reacted?

  (Slower to realise that Mr T is a throwback to an earlier period than contemporary readers would probably have been.)

- What is there about your own education and real or imagined experience which makes you respond the way you do to the text?

  (I love Dickens – so what some readers might find too long-winded, I really enjoy. They might think that the ways he puts ideas into Esther's mind that this rather bland character would probably never think – like seeing creases in the whites of Mr T's eyes – is a weakness. It just makes me laugh!)

Forming your own informed, independent opinions

- How has your reading of the text changed, once you have read it and thought about it several times?

- How has your view of the text and its possible meanings changed after discussing it with others, and after reading what other people have thought about it?

Assignments

Single texts

1 Look again at the extract from *The Canterbury Tales*, and at the critical responses to Chaucer in Part 4: Critical approaches (pages 33–34, and pages 102–103).

   Write a commentary on the extract, concentrating on one of the following focuses:
   - the language and poetry
   - the realism and universality
   - Chaucer's technique as narrator: his voice, use of detail, moral values and comment.

2 Look again at the extract from *The Rape of the Lock* (page 57), and the language and imagery used in it.

How would you interpret this passage if you were:
- a militant feminist
- a devout Roman Catholic
- a man with strictly puritanical moral values
- a working class girl?

Comparing texts

It is often easier to compare different texts than to focus exclusively on one. The following assignments take groups of texts from Part 3: Texts and extracts and combine them in different ways. The prompts suggest possible frameworks for thinking about their similarities and differences, and can be used either as a basis for discussion, or as preparation for writing.

3 Compare and contrast the ways in which these four writers deal with a religious topic:

   Chaucer's portrait of the Pardoner (pages 33–34)
   Skelton's depiction of Hampton Court (pages 37–38)
   Swift in 'A Meditation upon a Broomstick' (pages 49–50)
   Clough in 'The Latest Decalogue' (pages 77–78).

   You will find it helpful to think about:
   - the ideas and attitudes each extract reveals
   - the effects achieved by each writer's uses of language
   - the writers' attitudes to religion and the church
   - the ways in which these attitudes have changed over time
   - what the satirical butts (targets) are
   - the impact of the particular genre the writer has chosen to use (verse portrait in rhyming couplets; running rhymed short-lined verse; moral meditation in prose; rhyming hexameter couplets)
   - the tone and mood of each piece.

4 Look at the following passages:

   the extract from Ben Jonson's *The Alchemist* (pages 39–41)
   the extract from Congreve's *The Way of the World* (page 45–46)
   Pope's portrait of Belinda in *The Rape of the Lock* (page 57)
   E. E. Cummings' 'next to of course god' (page 85)
   the extract from Waugh's *Decline and Fall* (page 88).

Compare and contrast the writers' uses of form, structure and language in the five extracts, exploring the following aspects:
• your first impressions of these texts, what they are about and what they satirise
• the features which a critic interested in language (a linguistic critic) or in literary forms (a formalist or structuralist critic) would focus on. For example, the ways in which the writers use semantic fields (groups of words which relate together closely); the ways in which the language builds up a consistent frame of reference (alchemy, make up and vanity, jingoism, education)
• what these uses of language tell you about the tone of the piece
• what features in the writing denote the genre (poetic rhyming couplets; dramatic prose or verse; the sonnet; novelistic prose).

Now reread the five extracts and consider the following features:
• the aspects of these texts which seem to you to speak to whatever age the reader comes from
• the aspects of these texts which relate closely to the period and historical context from which they come
• the part the gender of the subject of the text, and of the writer, plays in determining your response
• what the attitude of the writer seems to be to what he is writing about, and what evidence you can find to support your ideas about this
• what a feminist, a moral or a social critic might make of these texts.

Having considered these aspects, what do you think is most interesting about the texts and how would you interpret them now?
     How and why does your view now vary from when you first considered these texts?

5   Look at the following:
         the extract from Skelton's *Colin Clout* (pages 37–38)
         the extracts from Dryden's *Absalom and Achitophel* (pages 43–44)
         the extracts from Swift's *A Modest Proposal* (pages 53–54)
         the extract from Pope's 'Epistle to Dr. Arbuthnot' (page 59).
These four extracts have often been thought to express strong feelings about their subjects. Consider them in the light of Pope's comment that 'to a true satirist nothing is so odious as a libeller'.

Consider:
- what seems to be intensely personal and how do you know?
- what words and phrases define the tone of each passage for you?
- what evidence of the writer's uses of form and structure can you find which suggest that the passage is 'art' rather than 'libel'?

Choose one of the extracts. You wish to demonstrate that this text is libellous. Prepare your argument, and supporting evidence.

Choose one of the extracts. You wish to demonstrate that this text is art, not libel. Prepare your argument, and supporting evidence.

The arguments can be presented orally to your group, and voted on, or used as the basis for further written work.

And finally:
- what contexts have you used in preparing your cases?
- what critical approaches have you used in preparing your cases?
- which of these passages do you think comes closest to libel and why?

6 From your work on the extracts in this book, what kinds of contextual knowledge have you found it most useful to seek out and bring to bear on satirical texts?

You could focus your answer on any whole texts which are forming part of your own wider reading, or on those represented in Part 3.

7 (a) Historically, there have been fewer female writers of satire, and in *The Anatomy of Satire* Gilbert Highet suggests that women find satire as a genre less enjoyable to read than men do.

From your reading of the extracts in Part 3, and any other satirical texts, how far do you agree or disagree with this view? What do you enjoy, or dislike, about satirical texts?

(b) Carol Ann Duffy has said recently that since the 1970s more and more women are producing satires.

Where in contemporary arts, literature and culture have you found women satirists at work? What are their targets, and how, in your opinion, does their work compare with that of male satirists?

6 | Resources

Satire 'trails'

These satire 'trails' have two purposes. The first is to encourage wider reading of satirical texts, by offering some further suggestions in addition to the texts from which the extracts in Part 3 have been chosen.

The second purpose is to try to indicate in a diagrammatic way the point made in Part 1 (page 13) about the origins of satire in the work of Horace on the one hand, and of Juvenal on the other. Originally the different qualities of these two writers led to different kinds of satirical work, varying in tone from ironic and humorous on Horace's side to denunciatory and critical on Juvenal's. These two strands persist in satirical writing, and it is possible to make a crude division between those satires in which the dominant tone is comic, and those in which the dominant tone is critical and judgmental. However, this crude division is not likely to be as useful to readers as trying to decide whether comedy or criticism seems to them to be uppermost in a specific text, or how these two elements have been blended in the text as a whole. Making this sort of decision, which is one about subtleties of emphasis rather than strictness of classification, will depend on the reader's own responses to the subject matter, the approach which the writer has adopted and the tone in which the text is written. It will also depend, to some extent, on the reader's awareness of the contexts in which the text was produced.

A different way of representing the possible variations in the handling of the comic and the critical in satirical texts might be to place them along a line running from 'the comic' at one end of the spectrum to 'the critical' at the other. You could then discuss where to place extracts from Part 3 or texts from the 'trails' along this line. Discussion on the almost inevitable differences of opinion about the positions of texts could help you to express your own informed opinions about satirical texts.

Satire 'trails'

tend to be comic

Horace

Chaucer

Morality plays

Comedy of humours

Jonson *Volpone; The Alchemist;*

Bartholomew Fair

Gay *The Beggar's Opera*

Restoration comedy

Comedy of manners

Congreve *The Way of the World*

Wycherley *The Country Wife*

Sheridan *School for Scandal;The Rivals*

Burns *Holy Willie's Prayer*

Jane Austen

Byron

Peacock

Thackeray *Vanity Fair*

Dickens

Huxley *Chrome Yellow; Antic Hay*

Waugh *Decline and Fall; Vile Bodies;*

Scoop

Joe Orton

Alan Ayckbourn

TV sitcom

Fawlty Towers

The Royle Family

tend to be critical

Juvenal

Skelton

Dryden

Pope

Swift

Johnson

Samuel Butler *The Way of All Flesh;*

Erewhon

Mark Twain

Orwell *Animal Farm; Nineteen*

Eighty Four

Shaw *The Doctor's Dilemma*

Tom Lehrer *songs*

Joseph Heller *Catch-22*

Jonathan Coe *What a Carve Up!*

That was the week that was

Beyond the Fringe

Private Eye

Caryl Churchill *Serious Money*

Spitting Image

Blackadder

Further reading

Cambridge Literature Series, including Ben Jonson *The Alchemist*, ed. Brian Woolland (Cambridge University Press, 1995)
The Resource Notes in the editions in this series contain useful contextual information, covering details about the writer's biography, the genre of the text, and its reception by contemporary and later readers.

Cambridge School Chaucer: The Pardoner's Tale, ed. Kirkham and Allen (Cambridge University Press, 2000)

Casebooks (Macmillan), with titles on Chaucer, Swift, Pope, Jane Austen, Byron
These consist of critical extracts, drawn from reviews written at the time of the publication of the texts and essays by critics from later periods.

Gilbert Highet *The Anatomy of Satire* (Princeton, New Jersey 1962)
James Sutherland *English Satire* (Cambridge University Press, 1959)
Two readable overviews of the development of satire in English literature.

James Leonard, Thomas Tenney, Thadious Davis (eds.) *Satire or Evasion? Black Perspectives on Huckleberry Finn* (Duke University Press, Durham and London, 1992)
Many examples of alternative readings of the same text. The final essay, by Arnold Rampersad, is a study of Twain's influence on later black American writers, women as well as men.

Brian Moon *Literary Terms: A Practical Glossary* (English and Media Centre, London, 1992)
Exactly what it says. A glossary of the main critical terminology, with illustrative examples and exercises to clarify their meaning and use.

Rob Pope *The English Studies Book* (Routledge, 1998)
An introduction to the theory and practice of contemporary English Studies, targeted at teachers and undergraduates. Intended to be used as a handbook, it contains accounts of major critical theories for reference, and an anthology of texts and textual activities to illustrate and develop understanding of these.

Martin Voigt *Swift in the Twentieth Century* (University of Utah, Detroit, 1964)
A useful summary of 20th-century critical approaches to Swift. Worth reading selectively to get a sense of how critics can change and develop their views over

time, as they come into contact with different theoretical ideas and apply them to their own reading.

Websites

Any search of the Internet will yield a growing number of sites under 'Satire', or under the names of the major figures and aspects of satire discussed in this book. Here are four sites that will lead you into literary, historical and visual areas of interest and importance:

http://encarta.msn.com/find/Concise.asp?ti=0079C000
A useful gateway offering a survey of satire from classical literature to the present day. Offers a helpful introduction and links to other sites.

http://www.adh.brighton.ac.uk/schoolofdesign/MA.COURSE/09/Lsatire.html
This is an excellent site for exploring the visual satire of the 18th century.

Two other sites that can be recommended for exploring satire and satirists in the 18th century:
http://www.teleport.com/~mgroves/18thCentury.htm
http://andromeda.rutgers.edu/~jlynch/18th/

Glossary

Authorial intention/intentionalist what the writer meant, or has said that she or he intended to mean, when writing the text.

Byronic hero the 'mean, moody and magnificent' hero of romantic literature, created by Byron, for example Mr Rochester, Heathcliff.

Caesura a pause near the middle of a line of verse, often found in 18th-century couplets, to give balance and sharpness to the sense.

Canon/canonical a list of major texts, regarded as essential to the study of a literature.

Canto a section, or part of a longer poem, comparable to a chapter in a novel.

Caricature an exaggerated representation of a person, in words or a picture, for comic or satirical effect.

Comedy of humours drama, mainly associated with Ben Jonson, which satirises the weaknesses in human nature, for example greed and gullibility in *The Alchemist*.

Comedy of manners drama which satirises the behaviour of upper class society, especially the unfaithfulness and deceptions of marriage partners.

Couplet a pair of rhymed lines of verse, of equal length. The heroic couplet has ten syllables, with five strong beats in each line. For example:

> But hark! the chiming clocks to dinner call;
> A hundred footsteps scrape the marble hall ...

The octosyllabic couplet has eight syllables, for example 'On the Death of Dr Swift', or 'The Latest Decalogue'.

Diatribe a sustained verbal attack (see also *Invective*).

Didactic intending to teach. The word often implies a rather heavy-handed moral message.

Epic a mythological or historical story of heroic actions, and struggles between good and evil, for example *The Odyssey, Beowulf, Paradise Lost.*

Form the overall shape or structure of a text. Forms may be traditional and follow strict rules, for example the sonnet; or original and determined by the writer to relate to and express the content of the text.

Genre a kind of writing. Sometimes used as the term for the three main kinds of literary text: prose, poetry or drama; sometimes refers to different types of text within these groups: thriller, gothic, lyric, comedy of manners.

Gothic (novels) novels dealing with the supernatural and the macabre, with appropriately sinister settings, endangered heroines and resourceful heroes.

Heroic couplet see *Couplet.*

Iambic pentameter a poetic line with ten syllables, five of them regularly accented, for example 'Beware of all, but most beware of man!'

Intertextuality echoes of, or references to, other texts, for example, Pope's uses of the names 'Ariel' and 'Timon' are intertextual references to characters in Shakespeare's plays.

Invective a violent verbal attack (see also *diatribe*).

Irony a way of writing or speaking in which the deeper meaning is different from, and often the opposite to, the literal meaning, for example Swift's *Modest Proposal.*

Lampoon a personal attack in verse, for example, Dryden on Shaftesbury.

Libel/libellous a published false statement, which damages a person's reputation.

Mock heroic a text which uses a serious model for satirical or comic purposes, by transforming significant events and heroic characters into insignificant and trivial ones, for example *The Rape of the Lock.*

Monologue a text with a single speaker.

Narrative the telling of a story. This may be done in many different ways: from inside the text, in the first person, through the voice of a character within the story;

or from outside the text, in the third person, by an omniscient (all-knowing), or an unreliable, narrator, who can explain characters' feelings and motivation.

Occasional verse   poetry prompted by a particular occasion, situation or person.

Oeuvre   the complete works of an author (from the French, meaning 'work')

Omniscient narrator   see *Narrative*.

Ottava rima   an eight-line verse, the first six lines rhyming alternately, and concluding with a rhyming couplet.

Parody   an imitation of the form or style of another text, or of another author's work.

Pastiche   writing in another author's style.

Persona   the speaker of a text, a character invented by the writer and not to be confused with the author, despite using the pronoun 'I', for example Colin in *Colin Clout*; the speaker in *A Modest Proposal*.

Picaresque   a narrative form which depends on a series of events, often during a journey, involving the central character of the text, for example *Don Juan, Decline and Fall*.

Reader response theory   the literary theory that emphasises the central role of the reader in making meanings from a text, and recognises that there can be no single correct interpretation of any text.

Sonnet   a poem of 14 lines, with a patterned rhyme scheme. There are several kinds of sonnet, often named after the writer who has made them most popular (Petrarchan, Shakespearean, Miltonic), which manage the 14 lines and the rhyme schemes differently. Despite its unconventional appearance, E. E. Cummings' 'next to of course god' is a conventional Petrarchan sonnet.

Stanza   another word for 'verse'. Both words mean the groups of lines in a poem, similar to paragraphs in prose. The words are interchangeable, but 'stanza' is more often used when writing about poetry written before 1900.

Vernacular   ordinary, everyday language.

Index

Acknowledgements

The authors and publishers wish to thank the following for permission to use copyright material:

Anvil Press Poetry Ltd for Carol Ann Duffy, 'Poet for Our Times' and 'Making Money' from *The Other Country* by Carol Ann Duffy (1990); Steve Bell for cartoon, 'Righty Ho!' included in *English and Media Magazine*, 27 (1993); Guardian News Service Ltd for Phillip Willan and John Ezard, 'Steps to heaven include giving up the booze', *The Guardian*, 18.9.99; Curtis Brown Group Ltd on behalf of the Estate of the author for material from Nevill Coghill, *The Canterbury Tales*. Copyright © 1951 Nevill Coghill; A M Heath & Co Ltd on behalf of the author and Random House UK Ltd for material from Joseph Heller, *Catch-22*. Copyright © Joseph Heller 1955; W W Norton & Company for E E Cummings, 'next to of course god america i', 'a salesman is an it that stinks Excuse' and 'ygUDuh' from *Complete Poems 1904–1962* by E. E. Cummings, ed. George J Firmage. Copyright © 1991 by the Trustees for the E.E.Cummings Trust and George James Firmage; The Peters Fraser and Dunlop Group Ltd on behalf of the Evelyn Waugh Trust for material from Evelyn Waugh, *Decline and Fall*. Copyright © Evelyn Waugh 1928.

Thanks are also due to the National Gallery for permission to reproduce *Marriage A-la-Mode*: IV 'The Countess's Morning Levee' by William Hogarth. Copyright © National Gallery, London.

Every effort has been made to reach copyright holders; the publishers would like to hear from anyone whose rights they have unknowingly infringed.